CONTENT-BASED IMAGE AND VIDEO RETRIEVAL

MULTIMEDIA SYSTEMS AND APPLICATIONS SERIES

Consulting Editor

Borko Furht
Florida Atlantic University

Recently Published Titles:

ELECTRONIC BUSINESS AND EDUCATION: ***Recent Advances in Internet Infrastructures***, edited by Wendy Chin, Frédéric Patricelli, Veljko Milutinović; ISBN: 0-7923-7508-4

INFRASTRUCTURE FOR ELECTRONIC BUSINESS ON THE INTERNET by Veljko Milutinović; ISBN: 0-7923-7384-7

DELIVERING MPEG-4 BASED AUDIO-VISUAL SERVICES by Hari Kalva; ISBN: 0-7923-7255-7

CODING AND MODULATION FOR DIGITAL TELEVISION by Gordon Drury, Garegin Markarian, Keith Pickavance; ISBN: 0-7923-7969-1

CELLULAR AUTOMATA TRANSFORMS: ***Theory and Applications in Multimedia Compression, Encryption, and Modeling***, by Olu Lafe; ISBN: 0-7923-7857-1

COMPUTED SYNCHRONIZATION FOR MULTIMEDIA APPLICATIONS, by Charles B. Owen and Fillia Makedon; ISBN: 0-7923-8565-9

STILL IMAGE COMPRESSION ON PARALLEL COMPUTER ARCHITECTURES, by Savitri Bevinakoppa; ISBN: 0-7923-8322-2

INTERACTIVE VIDEO-ON-DEMAND SYSTEMS: ***Resource Management and Scheduling Strategies***, by T. P. Jimmy To and Babak Hamidzadeh; ISBN: 0-7923-8320-6

MULTIMEDIA TECHNOLOGIES AND APPLICATIONS FOR THE 21st CENTURY: ***Visions of World Experts***, by Borko Furht; ISBN: 0-7923-8074-6

INTELLIGENT IMAGE DATABASES: ***Towards Advanced Image Retrieval***, by Yihong Gong; ISBN: 0-7923-8015-0

BUFFERING TECHNIQUES FOR DELIVERY OF COMPRESSED VIDEO IN VIDEO-ON-DEMAND SYSTEMS, by Wu-chi Feng; ISBN: 0-7923-9998-6

HUMAN FACE RECOGNITION USING THIRD-ORDER SYNTHETIC NEURAL NETWORKS, by Okechukwu A. Uwechue, and Abhijit S. Pandya; ISBN: 0-7923-9957-9

MULTIMEDIA INFORMATION SYSTEMS, by Marios C. Angelides and Schahram Dustdar; ISBN: 0-7923-9915-3

MOTION ESTIMATION ALGORITHMS FOR VIDEO COMPRESSION, by Borko Furht, Joshua Greenberg and Raymond Westwater; ISBN: 0-7923-9793-2

VIDEO DATA COMPRESSION FOR MULTIMEDIA COMPUTING, edited by Hua Harry Li, Shan Sun, Haluk Derin; ISBN: 0-7923-9790-8

CONTENT-BASED IMAGE AND VIDEO RETRIEVAL

by

Oge Marques
Borko Furht
Florida Atlantic University
Boca Raton, FL, U.S.A.

KLUWER ACADEMIC PUBLISHERS
Boston / Dordrecht / London

Distributors for North, Central and South America:
Kluwer Academic Publishers
101 Philip Drive
Assinippi Park
Norwell, Massachusetts 02061 USA
Telephone (781) 871-6600
Fax (781) 871-6528
E-Mail <kluwer@wkap.com>

Distributors for all other countries:
Kluwer Academic Publishers Group
Distribution Centre
Post Office Box 322
3300 AH Dordrecht, THE NETHERLANDS
Telephone 31 78 6392 392
Fax 31 78 6546 474
E-Mail <services@wkap.nl>

Electronic Services <http://www.wkap.nl>

Library of Congress Cataloging-in-Publication Data

A C.I.P. Catalogue record for this book is available
from the Library of Congress.

Printed on acid-free paper.

Printed in the United States of America

Contents

Preface

The main objective of this book is to excite the curiosity of its readers and inspire new technological breakthroughs in the exciting field of image and video retrieval systems.

Only a few years ago there was a small group of researchers and practitioners in the field of content-based image and video retrieval techniques. Today, this area has become one of the emerging areas of research in the multimedia field, with a large number of applications. These new applications, such as digital libraries, video-on-demand systems, geographic information systems, astronomical research, satellite observation systems, criminal investigation systems and others, need to store large collections of multimedia data consisting of images, video, and audio data. The challenge is to exploit these large multimedia databases by content.

Another challenge is the World Wide Web, which is a very large distributed information database. Most current search and retrieval systems use keywords only. However, in order to realize the full potential of the Web and search and retrieve multimedia data from the Web effectively requires adding the content-based retrieval techniques.

This book addresses the basic concepts and techniques for designing content-based image and video retrieval systems. It also discusses a variety of design choices for the key components of these systems. The book gives a comprehensive survey of the content-based image retrieval systems including several content-based video retrieval systems. The survey includes both research and commercial content-based retrieval systems. Finally, the book presents a detailed case study of designing MUSE — a content-based image retrieval system developed at Florida Atlantic University in Boca Raton, Florida.

The book also contains pointers to two hundred representative bibliographic references on this field — ranging from survey papers to description of recent work in the area, to entire books — and more than seventy Web sites.

A Web page for the book, containing color versions of representative images, updated useful links, and supplemental materials is available at: `http://www.cse.fau.edu/~omarques/CBIVRBook`.

OGE MARQUES AND BORKO FURHT

To my son Nicholas.

– Oge Marques

To my daughter Tanya.

– Borko Furht

Acknowledgments

Our thanks to Susan Lagerstrom-Fife and Jennifer Evans from Kluwer Academic Publishers, for their support to this project.

We are deeply indebted to Dr. Remco C. Veltkamp and Mirela Tanase, for contributing with their excellent and comprehensive survey to what became Chapter 5 of this book.

We would also like to acknowledge the support of our institution — Florida Atlantic University — and the funding provided by CAPES (Brasília-DF, Brazil) along the development of the MUSE Project, reported in Chapter 6.

Thanks to the members of the Visual Information Retrieval group at Florida Atlantic University.

Special thanks to James A. Russo, for his technical expertise, enthusiasm and willingness to always help, and Hugo Vieira Neto, for patiently reviewing earlier versions of portions of this manuscript.

Finally, and most importantly, a very heartfelt thank-you to our wives and children, for their constant support, encouragement, patience and understanding.

Chapter 1

INTRODUCTION

The amount of audiovisual information available in digital format has grown exponentially in recent years. Gigabytes of new images, audio and video clips are generated and stored everyday, helping to build up a huge, distributed, mostly unstructured repository of multimedia information, much of which can be accessed through the Internet.

Digitization, compression, and archiving of multimedia information have become popular and inexpensive, and there is a broad range of available hardware and software to support these tasks. Subsequent retrieval of the stored information, however, is not as straightforward and might require considerable additional work in order to be effective and efficient. There are basically three ways of retrieving previously stored multimedia data:

1 **Free browsing**: users browse through a collection of images, audio, and video files, and stop when they find the desired information.

2 **Text-based retrieval**: textual information (metadata) is added — either manually or using (semi-)automatic tools — to the audiovisual files during the cataloguing stage. In the retrieval phase, this additional information is used to guide conventional, text-based query and search engines to find the desired data.

3 **Content-based retrieval**: users search the multimedia repository providing information about the actual contents of the image, audio, or video clip. A content-based search engine translates this in-

formation in some way as to query the database[1] and retrieve the candidates that are more likely to satisfy the user's request.

The first two methods have several limitations. Free browsing is tedious, inefficient, and time-consuming and becomes completely impractical for large databases. Text-based search and retrieval suffers from two big problems associated with the cataloguing phase: (a) the considerable amount of time and effort needed to manually annotate each individual image or clip; and (b) the imprecision associated with the subjective human perception of the contents being annotated. These problems are aggravated when the multimedia collection gets bigger and may be the cause of unrecoverable errors in later retrieval.

Despite these problems, query by keyword is still the most popular method for searching visual information on the Web. Several general-purpose search engines have extended their capabilities to include keyword-based search of visual media. Examples include: Yahoo!'s Picture Gallery (`http://gallery.yahoo.com/`), the multimedia searcher of Lycos (`http://multimedia.lycos.com/`), and AltaVista Photofinder (`http://www.altavista.com/sites/search/simage`).

In order to overcome the inefficiencies and limitations of text-based retrieval of previously annotated visual data, many researchers, mostly from the Image Processing and Computer Vision community, started to investigate possible ways of retrieving visual information based solely on its contents. In other words, instead of being manually annotated using keywords, images and video clips would be indexed by their own visual content, such as color, texture, objects' shape and movement, among others. Research in the field of Content-Based Visual Information Retrieval (CBVIR) started in the early 1990's [135] and is likely to continue during the first decade of the 21st century. Many research groups in leading universities, research institutes, and companies ([22, 23, 28, 34, 36, 45, 61, 82, 96, 97, 109, 112, 116, 125, 126, 132, 133, 139, 158, 175], among many others) are actively working towards the ultimate goal of enabling users to retrieve the desired image or video clip among massive amounts of visual data in a fast, efficient, semantically meaningful, friendly, and location-independent manner.

Many improvements are still needed to move CBVIR solutions from research labs prototypes to the mainstream. At the time of this writing, the first commercial CBVIR systems are only starting to appear. They usually offer a product suite that performs a number of image or

[1]The use of the word *database* in the context of this dissertation is merely to mean a (large) collection of data. It does not necessarily mean that data is structured in any organized way.

video processing including filtering, indexing and classification, text and content-based retrieval, similarity search, and others.

An example of a commercial system is a product suite from LTU Technologies [106] that includes five products: Image-Filter, Image-Indexer, Image-Seeker, Image-Shopper, and Image-Watcher. The core of the LTU technology is a high-level perceptual image analyzer that is capable of indexing, recognizing, and describing images according to their visual features. The image analyzer consists of two steps: (1) Image segmentation, in which a complex image is divided into visual-relevant segments using a non-parametric, multiscale approach, and (2) Image indexing, in which the system assigns a unique identifier (or index) to the segmented image, called the signature, or content DNA. Image-Indexer uses the image analysis techniques to automate classification and semantic categorization of visual content. Image-Seeker performs similarity search within an image database to find a set of images similar to a particular image. The system also provides relevance feedback from the user to refine search results. Figure 1.1 illustrates how the Image-Seeker operates.

One of interesting new trends is the way of delivering commercial CVBIR systems. Besides offering their CBIVR system as a software product, some companies (such as Cobion and Virage) offer their CBIVR system as a service.

For example, in the case of Cobion [38], its customers purchase the service from Cobion, and then they offer it to their users. An example is illustrated in Figure 1.2. The heart of the Cobion's visual search platform is Global ImageCenter consisting of a parallel processing supercomputer with 1,000 processors. The system is capable of indexing and processing several millions images per day from the Web. The Cobion's customer (such as Infoseek) presents to its users its own Web site and the user starts the search. The customer's server then transforms the query to a HTTP request and send it to Cobion's server. Cobion's system performs search and retrieval and through Cobion's API returns a XML file. The customer's server then converts the results to a HTML file and presents to the user.

This book is organized as follows: Chapter 2 provides an overview of the fundamentals of CBVIR systems, primarily from a user's point of view. Chapter 3 takes a look behind the scenes and provides the necessary technical background on the main concepts, techniques, and technical challenges involved in designing and implementing a successful Content-Based Image Retrieval (CBIR) system. In Chapter 4 this discussion is extended to video. Chapter 5 provides a comprehensive survey of existing CBIR systems. Finally, Chapter 6 presents a detailed case study of designing MUSE — a content-based image retrieval system developed at Florida Atlantic University in Boca Raton, Florida.

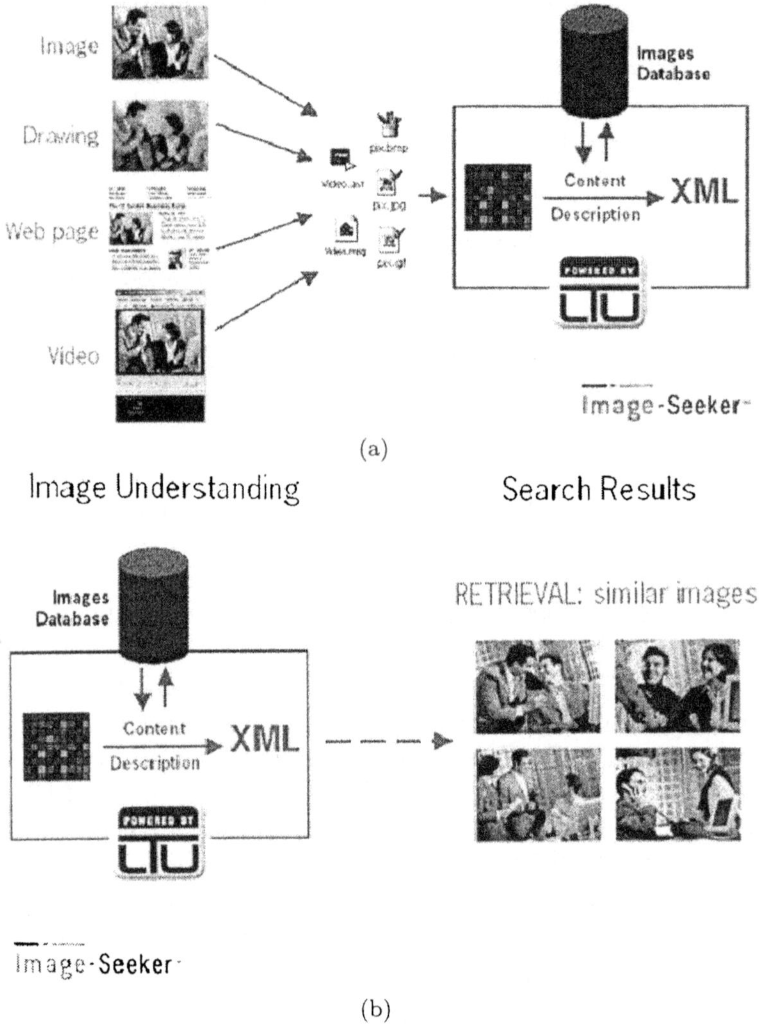

Figure 1.1. Image-Seeker: (a) An image is presented to the system and real-time image analysis is performed by extracting features of the image, (b) The system then matches these features with the features of images in the database and retrieves similar images (from [106]).

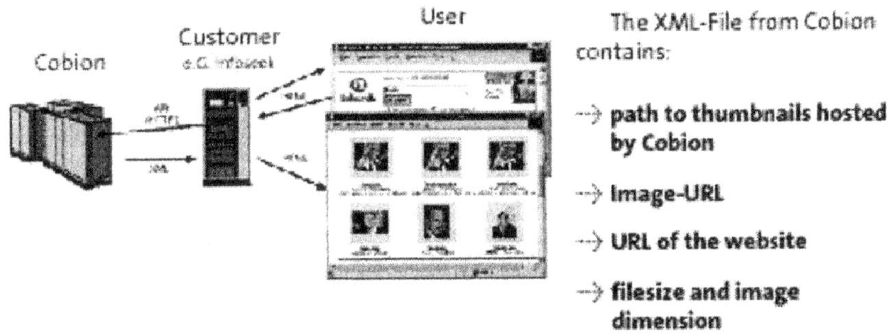

Figure 1.2. Cobion's visual search platform is based on the ASP approach. (From [38])

Chapter 2

FUNDAMENTALS OF CONTENT-BASED IMAGE AND VIDEO RETRIEVAL

This chapter contains basic information on Visual Information Retrieval (VIR) systems, particularly the ones whose primary emphasis is on searching for visual information (images or video clips)[1] based on their contents, which will henceforth be referred to as Content-Based Image and Video Retrieval (CBIVR) systems.

It introduces fundamental concepts, describes the main blocks of a CBIVR system, and discusses CBIVR systems from a user's perspective. A deeper discussion of design issues and related research work in this area is deferred to Chapter 3.

1. Basic Concepts

Visual Information Retrieval is a relatively new field of research in Computer Science and Engineering. As in conventional information retrieval, the purpose of a VIR system is to retrieve all the images that are relevant to a user query while retrieving as few non-relevant images as possible. The emphasis is on the retrieval of *information* as opposed to the retrieval of *data*. Similarly to its text-based counterpart, a VIR system must be able to interpret the contents of the documents (images) in a collection and rank them according to a degree of relevance to the user query. The interpretation process involves extracting semantic information from the documents (images) and using this information to match the user's needs [14].

[1] We shall use the expression 'image' to refer to visual information entities in general or static images in particular. For image sequences, expressions such as 'image sequence', 'video clip', or simply 'video' shall be used interchangeably.

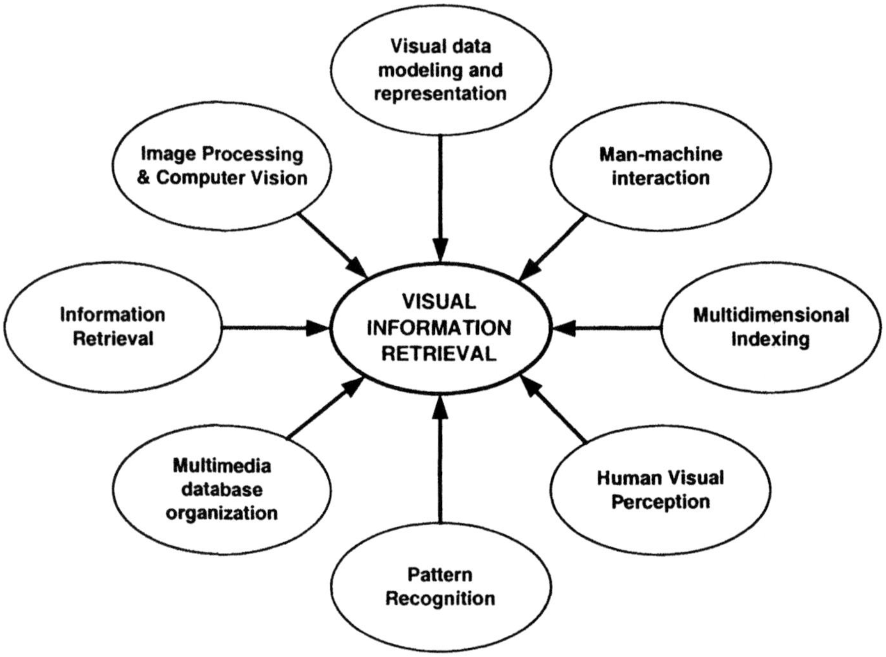

Figure 2.1. Visual Information Retrieval blends together many research disciplines.

Progress in Visual Information Retrieval has been fostered by recent research results in many fields (Figure 2.1), including: (text-based) information retrieval, image processing and computer vision, visual data modeling and representation, man-machine interaction, multidimensional indexing, human visual perception, pattern recognition, multimedia database organization, among others.

VIR systems can be classified in two main generations, according to the attributes used to search and retrieve a desired image or video file [49]:

- **First-generation VIR systems**: use query by text, allowing queries such as "all pictures of red Ferraris" or "all images of Van Gogh's paintings". They rely strongly on metadata, which can be represented either by alphanumeric strings, keywords, or full scripts, and can be obtained by manual input, transcripts, captions, embedded text, or hyperlinked documents. Their performance depend on the quality of the metadata, which can very often be incomplete, inaccurate, biased by the user's knowledge, ambiguous, or a combination of these.

- **Second-generation (CB)VIR systems**: support query by content, where the notion of content, for still images, includes, in increasing level of complexity: *perceptual properties* (e.g., color, shape, texture), *semantic primitives* (abstractions such as objects, roles, and scenes), and *subjective attributes* (such as impressions, emotions and meaning associated to the perceptual properties). The basic premise behind second-generation VIR systems is that images and videos are first-class entities and that users should be able to query their contents as easily as they query textual documents, without necessarily using manual annotation [73]. Many second-generation systems use content-based techniques as a complementary component, rather than a replacement, of text-based tools.

2. A Typical CBIVR System Architecture

Figure 2.2 shows a block diagram of a generic CBIVR system, whose main components are:

- **User interface**: friendly GUI that allows the user to interactively query the database, browse the results, and view the selected images or video clips.
- **Query / search engine**: collection of algorithms responsible for searching the database according to the parameters provided by the user.
- **Digital image and video archive**: repository of digitized, compressed images and video clips.
- **Visual summaries**: representation of image and video contents in a concise way, such as thumbnails for images or keyframes for video sequences.
- **Indexes**: pointers to images or video segments.
- **Digitization and compression**: hardware and software necessary to convert images and videos into digital compressed format.
- **Cataloguing**: process of extracting features from the raw images and videos and building the corresponding indexes.

Digitization and compression have become fairly straightforward tasks thanks to the wide range of hardware (cameras, scanners, frame grabbers, etc.) and software available. In many cases, images and videos are generated and stored directly in digital compressed format (typically using the standardized JPEG and MPEG compression schemes).

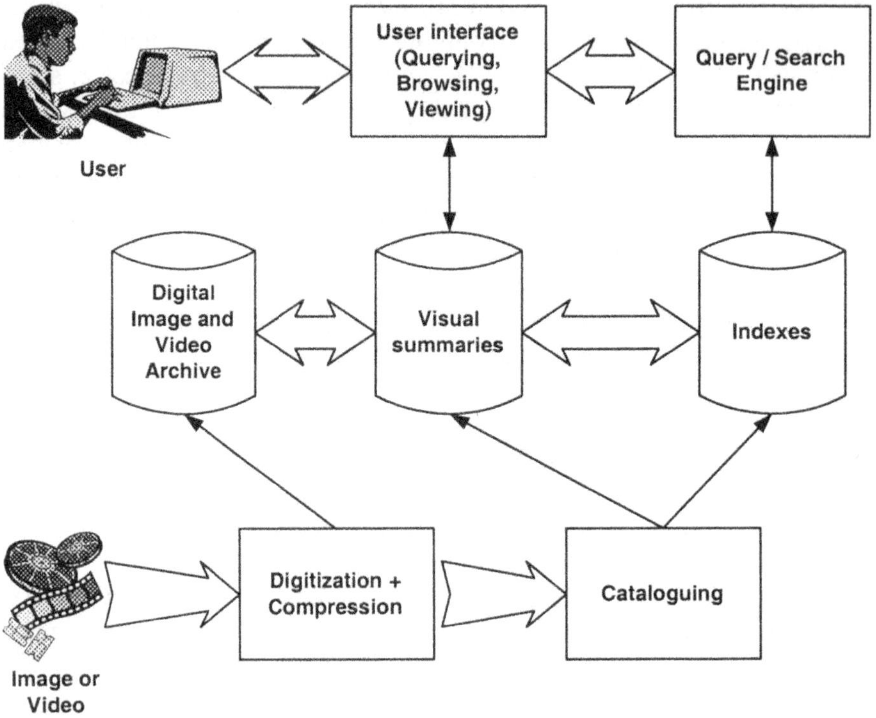

Figure 2.2. Block diagram of a CBIVR system.

For some specialized applications, however, the methods and devices currently used for these tasks are not suitable, and various alternative visual sensing mechanisms (stereo capture and analysis, 3-D scanners, etc.) and compression algorithms have been proposed to overcome these limitations.

The cataloguing stage is responsible for extracting features from the visual contents of the images and video clips. In the particular case of video, the original video segment is broken down into smaller pieces, called *scenes*, which are further subdivided into *shots*. Each meaningful video unit is indexed and a corresponding visual summary, typically a *key-frame*, is stored. In the case of images the equivalent process is known as *feature extraction*, which consists of extracting numerical information about the image contents. In either case, the cataloguing stage is also where metadata might be added to the visual contents. Manually adding metadata to image and video files is mandatory for text-based first-generation VIR systems. CBIVR systems, however, typically rely on minimum amount of metadata or none at all.

Digitization, compression, and cataloguing typically happen off-line. Once these three steps have been performed, the database will contain the image and video files themselves, possible simplified representations of each image file or video segment, and a collection of indexes that act as pointers to the corresponding images or video segments.

The online interaction between a user and a CBIVR system is represented on the upper half of the diagram in Figure 2.2. The user expresses her query using a GUI. That query is translated and a search engine looks for the index that corresponds to the desired image or video. The results are sent back to the user in a way that should allow easy browsing, viewing, and possible refinement of the query based on the partial results.

3. The User's Perspective

The user interface is a crucial component of a CBIVR system. Ideally such interface should be simple, easy, friendly, functional, and customizable. It should provide integrated browsing, viewing, searching, and querying capabilities in a clear and intuitive way. This integration is extremely important, since it is very likely that the user will not always pick the best match found by the query/search engine. More often than not users will want to check the first few best matches, browse through them, preview their contents, refine their query, and eventually retrieve the desired image or video segment.

Most VIR systems allow searching the visual database contents in several different ways — described below — either alone or combined:

- **Interactive browsing**: convenient to leisure users who may not have specific ideas about the images or video clips they are searching for. Clustering techniques can be used to organize visually similar images into groups and minimize the number of undesired images shown to the user.

- **Navigation with customized categories**: leisure users often find it very convenient to navigate through a subject hierarchy to get to the target subject and then browse or search that limited subset of images. The combination of navigation with customized categories followed by content-based search (within a category) has been proposed by several researchers ([30], for instance) who claim it can be the most effective mode of operation: in this case, the content-based portion of the VIR system would work on a smaller, semantically constrained, subset of images.

- **Query by X** [31], where 'X' can be:

- **an image example**: several systems allow the user to specify an image (virtually anywhere in the Internet) as an example and search for the images that are most similar to it, presented in decreasing order of similarity score. It is probably the most classical paradigm of image search. Many techniques have been developed over the past years to measure similarity between the example image (template) and the target images, but these techniques still have disadvantages such as sensitivity to noise and imaging conditions, and the need of a suitable example image.
- **a visual sketch**: some systems provide users with tools that allow drawing visual sketches of the image or video clip they have in mind. Users are also allowed to specify different weights for different features. Developers of one of these systems (VisualSEEk [156]) have observed, however, that "users are usually much less enthusiastic about this query method than others when the query interface is complex [30]."
- **specification of visual features**: direct specification of visual features (e.g., color, texture, shape, and motion properties) is possible in some systems and might appeal to more technical users.
- **a keyword or complete text**: some VIR systems rely on keywords entered by the user and search for visual information that has been previously annotated using that (set of) keyword(s).
- **a semantic class**: where users specify (or navigate until they reach) a category in a preexisting subject hierarchy.

We advocate that query options should be made as simple, intuitive and close to human perception of similarity as possible. Users are more likely to prefer a system that offers the "Show me more images that look similar to this" option, rather than a sophisticated interactive tool to edit that image's color histogram and perform a new search. While the latter approach might be useful for experienced technical users with image processing knowledge, it does not apply to the average user and therefore has limited usefulness. An ideal CBIVR system query stage should, in our opinion, hide the technical complexity of the query process from the end user. We agree with Gupta, Santini, and Jain, when they state that "A search through visual media should be as imprecise as 'I know it when I see it' [74]."

4. Summary

Visual Information Retrieval (VIR) is a new and dynamic field of research, with contributions from many areas of expertise, including:

(text-based) information retrieval, image processing and computer vision, human visual perception, pattern recognition, multimedia database organization, among others.

VIR systems can be classified in two main generations: first-generation VIR systems use query by text and rely strongly on metadata; second-generation (CB)VIR systems support query by content. Several VIR systems combine the use of content-based techniques with text-based tools. Current research has focused on improving second-generation systems in order to bridge the gap between the semantic meaning of an image or video scene and the raw information that is available from that image or video.

Most VIR systems allow searching the visual database contents in several different ways — either alone or combined — such as: interactive browsing, navigation with customized categories, query by example, query by visual sketch, specification of visual features, query by keyword, specification of a semantic class.

Chapter 3

DESIGNING A CONTENT-BASED IMAGE RETRIEVAL SYSTEM

This chapter provides a deeper foundation on the key components of a Content-Based Image Retrieval (CBIR) system and presents selected design questions faced by anyone who wishes to implement their own CBIR system.

1. Feature Extraction and Representation

CBIVR systems should be able to automatically extract visual features that are used to describe the contents of an image or video clip. Examples of such features include color, texture, size, shape, spatial information, and motion (in video).

The process of indexing an image database by the images' contents is known as *feature extraction*. Mathematically, each extracted feature is encoded in an n-dimensional vector — henceforth called *feature vector* — whose components are computed by image processing and analysis techniques and used to compare images against each other.

In specific contexts the process of feature extraction can be enhanced and/or adapted to detect other, specialized attributes, such as human faces or objects[1]. Because of perception subjectivity, there is no best representation for a given feature [135]. Feature extraction is a critical stage in any CBIVR system, because it is the one that performs the mapping between the raw contents of each image or video clip onto a numerical representation that can be used as an index to access that image or video. In other words, it is very difficult — if not at all impossible

[1]Section 1.5 contains a brief discussion of specialized features.

— for any indexing, clustering, or learning algorithm to make up for a poor feature extraction scheme.

1.1 Feature Classification and Selection

Features can be classified in three categories[2], according to the level of abstraction they represent:

1 **Low-level features**: visual cues, such as color or texture, extracted directly from the raw pixel values of an image.

2 **Middle-level features**: regions or blobs obtained as a result of image segmentation.

3 **High-level features**: semantic information about the meaning of an image, its objects and their roles, and categories to which the image belongs.

Low-level features can be extracted using current image processing and computer vision techniques, some of which are described along this chapter. Middle-level features require further processing whose full automatization is beyond the current state-of-the-art. High level features are even harder to extract without explicit human assistance [44]. At this moment, most CBIR systems rely only on low-level features [22, 23, 36, 45, 61, 97, 125, 126, 139, 158], while some use human-assisted techniques to identify regions or blobs [25, 109].

The selection of which low-level features to use when designing a CBIR system should obey the following criteria. A good low-level feature $f(\mathcal{I})$ for an image $\mathcal{I}$ should have certain qualities:

1 **perceptual similarity**: the distance between feature vectors from two images $\mathcal{I}$ and $\mathcal{I}'$, $d(f(\mathcal{I}),f(\mathcal{I}'))$, should provide an accurate measure of the dissimilarity between the two images.

2 **efficiency**: $f(\mathcal{I})$ should be fast to compute.

3 **economy**: $f(\mathcal{I})$ should be small in size.

Perceptual similarity determines the effectiveness of a feature for the purpose of image retrieval. This is hard to achieve using only low-level features. For example, the two pairs of images shown in Figure 3.1 are very similar to the human eye in most aspects (color, shape, texture,

[2]There is no consensus in the literature about this. Other different categories for image features can be found, such as the one proposed by [64].

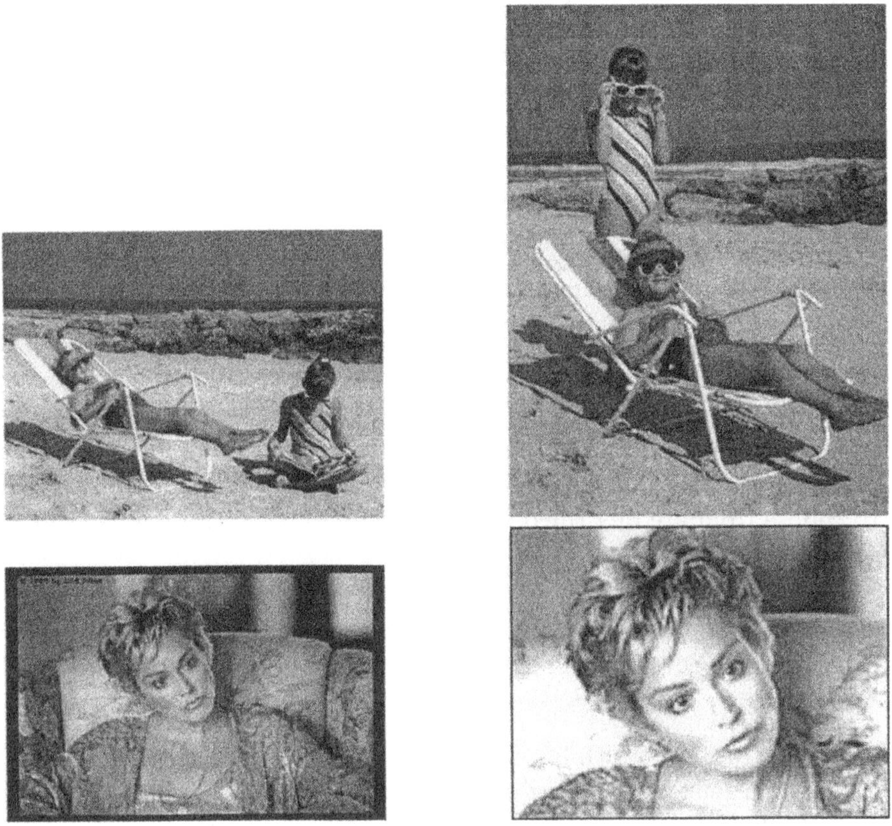

Figure 3.1. Two pairs of perceptually similar images.

semantic meaning), but a color histogram-based image retrieval system would rank the images to the right as the 61st and 2545th more similar to the ones to the left, respectively, in a database with more than 11,000 images.

Other desirable and important properties of an image feature are **stability** and **scalability**. Stability refers to the capacity of tolerating significant image changes and still perceive images as similar. Scalability measures how insensitive to the size of the image database a given feature is. Some feature extraction algorithms perform fairly well for small databases but fail to do so for bigger image collections because the features become more prone to false matches.

1.2 Color-Based Features

"Color is one of the most obvious and pervasive qualities in our environment [62]." It is also a dominant feature in any CBIVR system. Among its advantages we can mention:

- Robustness to background complications.
- Independence of size and rotation.
- Meaningfulness to human beings.

Selecting a powerful yet economic color-based feature extraction method is an important step in the design of a CBIVR system. There are many choices to be made, from the color model to the method for extraction of color information to the dissimilarity measure adopted to compare two images according to their color contents. Some of the many options to choose from are described next.

1.2.1 Color Models

Color stimuli are commonly represented as points in three-dimensional color spaces. Several color models have been proposed over the years. They can be classified as [49]:

- **Colorimetric models.** They result from physical measurements of spectral reflectance using colorimeters. A well-known example is the CIE chromaticity diagram.
- **Physiologically inspired models.** They rely on results from neurophysiology and take into account the existence of three different types of cones in the human retina, one for each primary color, red, green, and blue. The CIE XYZ and the RGB models belong to this category.
- **Psychological models.** They are based on how colors appear to a human observer. The hue-saturation-brightness family of models belong to this group.

Color models can also be differentiated as:

- **Hardware-oriented models.** They are defined according to the properties of devices used to capture or display color information, such as scanners, monitors, TV sets, and printers. Examples include the RGB, CMY(K), and YIQ models.
- **User-oriented models.** They are based on current knowledge about the human perception of colors, which states that humans perceive

colors through hue, saturation, and brightness percepts. *Hue* describes the actual wavelength of the color percept. *Saturation* describes the amount of white light present in a color. *Brightness* (also called value, intensity, or lightness) represents the intensity of a color. The HLS, HCV, HSV, HSB, MTM, L*u*v*, and L*a*b* models belong to this class.

Furthermore, color spaces can also be classified as *uniform* or *non-uniform*. Uniform color spaces are spaces such that a color difference perceived by a human observer is approximated as the Euclidean distance between two points in the color space. Examples include the MTM, L*u*v*, and L*a*b* models. The HSV family of models is the best-known example of non-uniform color spaces.

Here is a brief description of the most widely used color models[3]:

- **CIE chromaticity diagram**[4]. A tool for color definition conceived by the *Commission Internationale de l'Eclairage* (CIE) that reveals that almost any spectral composition can be achieved by a suitably chosen mix of three monochromatic primaries (lights of a single wavelength), namely, red, green, and blue. It does not correspond to any hardware device, nor to the way the human vision perceives color.

- **RGB**. The most commonly used hardware-oriented color scheme for digital images. It preserves compatibility with the devices that originate or display images and is somewhat based on the physiology of the human retina. The RGB color space is represented as a unit cube.

- **CMY(K)**. The CMY color space is used for color printing. It is based on the three subtractive primary colors, Cyan, Magenta, and Yellow. Since most color printers are equipped with a black (K) cartridge in addition to the inks corresponding to the three primary colors, the model is sometimes referred to as CMYK.

- **HSV**. The HSV (Hue-Saturation-Value) color model is part of a family of non-uniform color spaces, containing other similar models such as HIS (or HSI), HCV, HSB, and HLS[5]. It is usually represented as a double cone (Figure 3.2). The axis of the cone is the intensity/value scale. Gray is in the middle of the axis, white in the top cone vertex,

[3]For an interesting online exhibit of color representation models and diagrams dating back to the 16th Century, please refer to [3].

[4]Also referred to as **CIEXYZ** in the literature.

[5]The literature is rather confusing about these variants of the HSV color model. Different references use different names/acronyms and very few describe their details to a level that allows establishing a clear distinction among them.

an black in the bottom cone vertex. Hue is represented by the angle around the vertical axis. Saturation is represented by the distance from the central axis. More saturated colors are located towards the maximum circle. Primary colors are located on the maximum circle, equally spaced at 60 degrees.

- **YIQ**. The YIQ color model is used by the NTSC television standard. It was originally conceived to allow compatibility between existing black-and-white TV systems (whose signal is represented by the luminance component, Y) and the new color TV systems. The color information is encoded in two additional components, I (which roughly corresponds to $red - cyan$) and Q (which can be interpreted as $magenta - green$).

- **MTM**. The MTM (Mathematical Transform to Munsell) is a perceptually uniform color space that approximates the model first proposed by Munsell late in the 19th century and can easily be obtained from RGB values.

- **L*u*v***[6]. Device-independent model adopted by CIE in 1960 to minimize some problems with the original CIEXYZ model, particularly the disparity between the degree of perceptual difference (or similarity) between two colors and the corresponding distances (line lengths) in the CIEXYZ diagram.

- **L*a*b***[7]. Model adopted by CIE in 1976 that uses an opponent color system. Color opposition correlates with discoveries in the mid-1960s that somewhere between the optical nerve and the brain, retinal color stimuli are translated into distinctions between light and dark, red and green, and blue and yellow. CIELAB indicates these values with three axes: L*, a*, and b*. The central vertical axis represents lightness (L*) whose values run from 0 (black) to 100 (white). The color axes are based on the fact that a color cannot be both red and green, or both blue and yellow, because these colors oppose each other. On each axis the values run from positive to negative. On the a-a' axis, positive values indicate amounts of red while negative values indicate amounts of green. On the b-b' axis, yellow is positive and blue is negative. For both axes, zero is neutral gray.

[6] Also referred to as **CIELUV** in the literature.
[7] Also referred to as **CIELAB** in the literature.

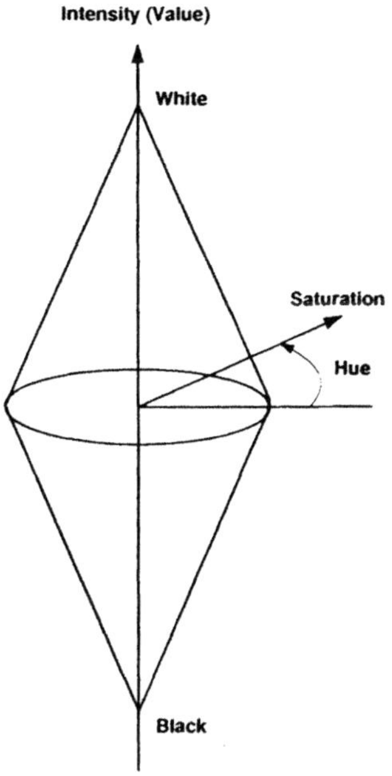

Figure 3.2. The HSV color model.

1.2.2 Representation of Color Properties

After having chosen a color model, the next step is to decide on how to represent the color contents of an image according to that model. Some of the best-known methods for color representation are:

- **Color histogram** [165]. The color histogram is the most traditional way of representing low-level color properties of images. It can be represented as three independent color distributions, one for each primary, or — more frequently — as one distribution over the three primaries, obtained by discretizing image colors and counting how many pixels belong to each color. Histograms are invariant to translations and rotation about the viewing axis, and change only slowly under change of angle of view, change in scale and occlusion. However, histograms, by themselves, do not include spatial information, so that images with very different layouts may have the same histogram.

- **Color names**. Names distinguish colors in a spoken language [62]. Associating names to colors permits the creation of mental images of the colors referred to. Color names are taken from a dictionary of names, associated with basic colors according to a naming system. Each mapping has a confidence measure associated with the degree to which the name is considered representative of the color. A possible way to define a model of color naming is to partition the color space and assign each piece to a color name.

- **Color moments**. Originally conceived by Stricker and Orengo [163], this color representation method proposes the storage of the first three central moments of the probability distribution of each color. The first moment conveys information about the average color of the image, while the second and third moments represent the variance and skewness of each color channel. In order to compare two images according to their color moments, they propose a similarity function that consists of a weighted sum of the absolute differences of the moments summed over all color channels.

All the methods above suffer from a common problem: although they summarize the global color properties of an image, they fail to encode spatial information about where pixels having a particular color are located and how they relate to other pixels in the image. Several methods have been recently proposed that use a combination of color features and spatial relations, among which we cite:

- **Division of the image in sub-blocks and extraction of color features from each sub-block**. Although natural and conceptually simple, this approach — with many variants, such as the one published in [35] — cannot provide accurate local color information and is computation- and storage-expensive.

- **Color coherence vector (CCV)**. Pass, Zabih, and Miller [131] have proposed a method to take into account spatial information in color images that labels each pixel as coherent or incoherent, as to a given color. Pixel sets are determined as the maximal sets, such that every pixel in the set has, at least, a pixel of the same color among its eight neighbors. Moreover, the size of the set must exceed a fixed threshold — a region is classified as coherent if its size is about 1 percent of the size of the image. For each color — taken from a discretized set of colors — the total number of coherent (α) and incoherent (β) pixels are computed. The image coherence vector is defined as:

$$V_C = [(\alpha_1, \beta_1), ..., (\alpha_n, \beta_n)] \tag{3.1}$$

  where n is the number of bucketed colors.

CCVs are compared according to the following metric:

$$D_c(I_Q, I_D) = \sum_{j=1}^{n} (|\alpha_{Qj} - \alpha_{Dj}| + |\beta_{Qj} - \beta_{Dj}|) \quad (3.2)$$

- **Color correlogram.** The main limitation of the color histogram approach is its inability to distinguish images whose color distribution is identical, but whose pixels are organized according to a different layout. The color correlogram, a feature originally proposed by Huang [85, 86], overcomes this limitation by encoding color-spatial information into (a collection of) co-occurrence matrices. Each entry (i, j) in the co-occurrence matrix expresses how many pixels whose color is C_j can be found at distance d from a pixel whose color is C_i. Each different value of d leads to a different co-occurrence matrix. Because the storage requirements for a co-occurrence matrix are too big, only its main diagonal is computed and stored, which is known as the *autocorrelogram*.

- **Color sets.** Technique proposed by Smith and Chang and used in the VisualSEEk system [155, 156, 157, 158] to locate regions within a color image. Color sets are binary vectors that correspond to a selection of colors. It is assumed that salient image regions have only a few dominant colors. The number of pixels belonging to each salient region must be greater than a certain threshold and the spatial segments of the region must be connected. Each color should be at least 20 per cent of the total. Colors are represented in the HSV space.

1.2.3 Other Parameters

Choosing a color model and a compatible method for extracting color information is only part of the process. Each specific color extraction method will have a number of parameters whose values may significantly impact performance. Here are a few examples:

- Number of bins in color histogram and color correlogram: increasing the number of bins leads to a richer color representation (and the capacity of distinguishing more subtle nuances of colors), at the expense of larger storage space and longer processing time.

- Distances in color correlogram: the distance set used in the color correlogram technique poses another trade-off between storage and computation requirements versus expressiveness of the results.

- The use of a color constancy / normalization algorithm: color constancy is a remarkable property of the human visual system [62] that is very hard to emulate in artificial vision systems. Several attempts to minimize the dependency on the average brightness of a scene have been proposed, from very simple [166] to fairly complex [59] algorithms.

1.2.4 Additional Remarks

Color image processing is a fairly young area of research, that has benefited from the explosive growth in the number of powerful affordable color devices — from digital cameras to printers — over the past decade.

The advent and popularization of these devices — along with several other factors — has fostered the use of color in image processing and pattern recognition problems. Color features make some of these problems much simpler compared to when only shape, texture, and intensity information are available.

However, the gap between machine-level processing of color information and human perception of color has not been fully bridged yet. Many human factors might play a significant role in the way we detect, process, and compare images according to their color contents. Here are some examples of aspects of human color perception that might be subject of further studies as we try to improve the performance of color-based artificial vision systems:

- Humans in general have a biased perception of colors [146]. For example, wall colors are generally unsaturated pastels and not saturated colors; reds tend to stimulate, while blues tend to relax.

- It is estimated that 8% of humans have some kind of color blindness [146], meaning that color combinations should be chosen carefully for effective communication.

- The human eye is capable of performing chromatic adaptation, a process that can be used in explaining — at least partially — our color constancy capacity.

- An object's perceived color is affected not only by the observer's state of adaptation, but also by the object's surroundings.

Various theories have been proposed to explain color processing in terms of processing by neurons. This higher-level processing is not fully understood and human visual processing is constantly under study. It is possible that advances in the fields of psychology and physiology of vision will help improving the quality of computer vision techniques for color perception.

1.3 Texture-Based Features

Texture is a powerful discriminating feature, present almost everywhere in nature. Texture similarity, however, is more complex than color similarity. Two images can be considered to have similar texture when they show similar spatial arrangements of colors (or gray levels), but not necessarily the same colors (or gray levels).

There are several possible approaches to represent and extract the texture properties of an image. Different authors use different classifications. According to Gonzalez and Woods [66], there are three main categories of texture models:

1 **Statistical models**. Statistical approaches to describe texture properties usually fall within one of these categories:

- The use of statistical moments of the gray-level histogram of an image or region to describe its texture properties. The second moment (the variance) is of particular importance because it measures gray-level contrast and can therefore be used to calculate descriptors of relative smoothness. Histogram information can also be used to provide additional texture measures, such as *uniformity* and *average entropy*. Similarly to what was said for color histograms as color descriptors, the main limitation of using histogram-based texture descriptors is the lack of positional information.
- The use of descriptors (energy, entropy, contrast, homogeneity, etc.) derived from the image's gray-level co-occurrence matrix, originally proposed by [80].

2 **Spectral models**. Rely on the analysis of the power spectral density function in the frequency domain. Coefficients of a 2-D transform (e.g., the Wavelet transform [33, 71, 100]) may be considered to indicate the correlation of a brightness pattern in the image. Coarse textures will have spectral energy concentrated at low spatial frequencies, while fine textures will have larger concentrations at high spatial frequencies.

3 **Structural models**. Methods that suggest describing texture in terms of primitive *texels* [146] in some regular or repeated relationship. This approach is appealing for artificial, regular patterns.

Texture is a broad concept, involving aggregations that often depend on data, context, and culture. Moreover, it is fundamentally a problem of scale, and that is why it is so difficult to find texture descriptors that work well in unconstrained databases (as opposed to specialized texture databases, such as the Brodatz texture collection [2]).

1.4 Shape-Based Features

Color and texture are both global attributes of an image. Shape goes one step further and typically requires some kind of region identification process to precede the shape similarity measure process. In other words, an image must be segmented into meaningful objects and background before applying most shape descriptors. In many cases this has to be done manually, but in restricted domains automatic segmentation is possible. Segmentation of "difficult" scenes is an open problem in computer vision [146].

Shape representation techniques can be classified in three broad categories [49]:

1 **Feature-vector approach**. In this case, a shape is represented as a numerical feature vector whose elements are the prominent attributes of the shape.

2 **Relational approach**. Methods in this category break down a shape into a set of salient component parts. These are individually described through suitable features. The overall description includes both the descriptors of the individual parts and the relations between them.

3 **Shape through transformations**. Shapes can also be distinguished by measuring the effort needed to transform one shape into another.

It is very hard to perform accurate and meaningful shape-based similarity comparisons without resorting to segmentation. Segmentation in an unconstrained context is difficult, and sometimes meaningless. As a consequence of these two facts, the contribution of shape in a general purpose CBIVR systems working on unconstrained databases has been modest.

1.5 Specialized Features

Although most of the efforts in current VIR system development has been concentrating on color, texture, and shape, these are not the entities that a user has in mind when performing a search. Users might be interested in objects, such as people or dogs, or even more abstract concepts, such as poverty or happiness.

Some VIR systems have experimented with specialized features and their use to detect specific objects or concepts. Examples include: face finding [118], flesh finding[8] [55], and retrieval by objects and their spatial relationships [51].

2. Similarity Measurements

After the color, shape, or texture information is extracted from an image, it is normally encoded into a feature vector. Given two feature vectors, $\mathbf{x}_1$ and $\mathbf{x}_2$, a distance function computes the difference between them. It is hoped that this difference will accurately measure the dissimilarity between the images from which the features were extracted. The greater the distance, the less the similarity. Commonly used distance functions are the Euclidean (L_2) norm and the city-block metric (also known as Manhattan distance or L_1 norm), whose equations follow:

- Euclidean distance:

$$d_E(\mathbf{x}_1, \mathbf{x}_2) = \sqrt{\sum_{i=1}^{i=n} (\mathbf{x}_1[i] - \mathbf{x}_2[i])^2} \tag{3.3}$$

- Manhattan distance:

$$d_M(\mathbf{x}_1, \mathbf{x}_2) = \sum_{i=1}^{i=n} |\mathbf{x}_1[i] - \mathbf{x}_2[i]| \tag{3.4}$$

Distance functions or metrics observe the following properties:

$$d(p, q) >= 0 \quad (d(p, p) = 0) \tag{3.5}$$

$$d(p, q) = d(q, p) \tag{3.6}$$

and

$$d(p, z) <= d(p, q) + d(q, z) \tag{3.7}$$

Specific feature extraction methods might introduce new similarity measures, such as the *histogram intersection*, proposed by [166] and used to compare color histograms:

$$H(\mathbf{x}_1, \mathbf{x}_2) = \frac{\sum_{i=1}^{i=n} \min(\mathbf{x}_1[i], \mathbf{x}_2[i])}{\sum_{i=1}^{i=n} \mathbf{x}_1[i]} \tag{3.8}$$

There is a great deal of controversy about how well metric distance functions measure human perceptual judgments about visual similarity.

[8]Used in automatic detection and filtering of objectionable images based on the amount of nudity they contain.

Recent research in computer vision and cognitive science indicate that those judgments are inherently non-metric, i.e., they may not obey the triangle inequality (Equation 3.7). Jacobs and others [88] have proposed and tested non-metric similarity measures for image classification.

3. Dimension Reduction and High-dimensional Indexing

After the features have been extracted and grouped into some suitable data structure or mathematical construct (e.g., a normalized feature vector), one of the main challenges is the high dimensionality of the feature vectors (typically of the order of 10^2). Solutions to the high dimensional indexing problem include reducing the dimension of the feature vectors and the use of efficient multi-dimensional indexing techniques.

When dealing with very large image databases it might become impractical to linearly search the whole database for images that satisfy a given query. Instead, the images must be organized and indexed so that only a fraction of them are considered during a query. Index structures ideally filter out all irrelevant messages while retaining the relevant images, which are then ranked in order of similarity according to a query.

Text-based VIR systems can rely on conventional indexing techniques for textual information, such as hash tables and signature files. CBIVR systems, however, must employ some type of indexing of visual attributes, which have been the subject of much recent research. Among the proposed solutions to the problem, we mention: K-d trees and their variants [18, 185], R-trees and their variants [16, 75, 143], and SS-trees [186], among many others.

4. Clustering

Clustering is the process of grouping the data into classes or clusters so that objects within a cluster have high similarity in comparison to one another, but are very dissimilar to objects in other clusters [78]. Clustering is a widely used approach for unsupervised learning in Pattern Recognition, Data Mining, and related areas.

The motivation for using clustering in CBIR systems stems from two different reasons:

- From a visual perception point of view, it is expected that clustering the feature vectors obtained as the result of a particular feature extraction module would group together images that look alike according to that feature.

- From a computational standpoint, dealing with clusters instead of individual images while performing the required calculations in each iteration, should reduce the time spent on those calculations by at least one order of magnitude.

One of the biggest challenges in using clustering to group visually similar images is to find a feature vector–clustering algorithm combination that provides visually meaningful results. This problem has been addressed by [8, 65, 95], among others. It becomes even bigger when one tries to accommodate heterogeneous features (such as color, texture, and shape) together. This problem has been discussed in [147], where a solution — called *semantic clustering* — is proposed.

5. The Semantic Gap

The human perception of visual contents is strongly associated to high-level, semantic information about the scene. Current computer vision techniques work at a lower level (as low as individual pixels). CBIR systems that rely on low-level features only can answer queries such as:

- Find all images that have 30% of red, 10% of orange and 60% of white pixels, where orange is defined as having a mean value of red = 255, green = 130, and blue = 0.
- Find all images that have a blue sky above a green grass.
- Find all images that are rotated versions of this particular image.

In general, the user is looking for higher-level semantic features of the desired image, such as "a beautiful rose garden", "a batter hitting a baseball", or "an expensive sports car". There is no easy or direct mapping between the low-level features and the high-level concepts. The distance between these two worlds is normally known as *semantic gap.*

There are two ways of minimizing the semantic gap. The first consists of adding as much metadata as possible to the images, which was already discussed and shown to be impractical. The second suggests the use of user relevance feedback (see section 7) combined with learning algorithms to make the system understand and learn the semantic context of a query operation.

6. Learning

The exact definition of (machine) learning is subject of much controversy. While the conventional interpretation of learning as "acquiring knowledge by experience, study, or being taught" might be satisfactory for many, some authors claim that a more operational definition of (machine) learning associates learning with "changes in behavior in a way that makes [a system] perform better in the future", hence tieing learning to *performance* rather than *knowledge* [187].

In the broader sense of CBIVR we believe that both performance improvement and knowledge acquisition can be achieved using machine learning techniques. Systems that work basically on target searching mode — such as MUSE, described in Chapter 6 — may experience performance improvements (e.g., number of iterations needed to reach the target) as a consequence of learning the user's preferences along a session. Systems that use some type of categorization — such as the ones that try to distinguish indoor from outdoor scenes [168] — might demonstrate actual knowledge after having learned what each type of scene should contain to be classified as such.

7. Relevance Feedback (RF)

Early attempts in the field of CBIVR aimed at fully automated, open-loop systems. It was hoped that current computer vision and image processing techniques would be good enough for image search and retrieval. The modest success rates experienced by such systems encouraged researchers to try a different approach, emphasizing interactivity and explicitly including the human user in the loop. An example of this shift can be seen in the work of MIT Media Lab researchers in this field, when they moved from the "automated" Photobook [132] to the "interactive" FourEyes [116].

The expression *relevance feedback* has been used to describe the process by which a system gathers information from its users about the relevance of features, images, image regions, or partial retrieval results obtained so far. Such feedback might be provided in many different ways and each system might use it in a particular manner to improve its performance. The expected effect of relevance feedback is to "move" the query in the direction of relevant images and away from the non-relevant ones [60, 61]. Relevance feedback has been used in contemporary CBIR systems, such as FourEyes [116], MARS [129, 136, 137, 138, 139, 141], and PicHunter [41, 42, 43, 44, 45], among others.

In CBVIR systems that support relevance feedback a search typically consists of a query followed by repeated user feedback, where the user comments on the items that were retrieved. The use of relevance feedback makes the user interactions with the system simpler and more natural. By selecting images, image regions, and/or image features, the user is in one way or another telling the system what he wants without the burden of having to describe it using sketches or keywords, for instance.

There are many ways of using the information provided by the user interactions and refining the subsequent retrieval results of a CBIVR system. One approach concentrates on the query phase and attempts to use the information provided by relevance feedback to refine the queries. Another option is to use relevance feedback information to modify feature weights, such as in the MARS project [129, 136, 137, 138, 139, 141]. A third idea is to use relevance feedback to construct new features on the fly, as exemplified by [117]. A fourth possibility is to use the relevance feedback information to update the probability of each image in a database being the target image, in other words, to predict the goal image given the user's interactions with the system. The latter is the approach taken by Cox et al. [41, 42, 43, 44, 45] in the PicHunter project.

8. Benchmarking CBVIR Solutions

Benchmarking visual information retrieval solutions is an open problem and the research community is still debating on how to come up with a suite of images, a set of queries, and evaluation criteria for that purpose [101]. While a standardized way of comparing two solutions against each other is not yet available, each system relies on its own set of quantitative (e.g., recall, precision, response time) and qualitative measures. Here is a summary of the latest recommendations issued by the Technical Committee 12 [1] from the International Association for Pattern Recognition (IAPR) regarding benchmarking for Visual Information Retrieval:

1 An extensible suite of benchmarks that consist of a number of component sets that cater for different applications requirements should be developed.

2 The resultant image collections must be freely available to researchers to experiment on, and free from any conditions or restrictions.

3 To minimize dependence on hardware and other extraneous factors, the entire image collection in question should be stored in main memory during the evaluation. The main aim is to test the ability of the algorithms to retrieve visual information.

4 The initial number of images in the object-based photograph category should be 1,000, which may be scaled up at a later stage.

5 The photographic images should contain multi-object, with diverse relationships existing among the objects, where the objects and relationships should also include a variety of qualifying attributes (In

MPEG-7, it is well acknowledged that a keyword approach will not be adequate, particularly for this type of images).

6 The images should be in JPEG format.

7 A set of 20 evaluation queries which cover a representative cross-section of contents should be designed against the 1,000 photographic images.

8 The queries should be based solely on the visual contents of the images. In particular, retrieval based on metadata should not be used. In the case of the object-based photographs, queries based solely on primitive contents should not be used.

9 For each query, there should be known answers that do not exceed 15 images (a percentage may be specified instead, e.g. 1.5%).

10 Images returned for possible browsing should not be greater than 15 at any stage.

11 The measures to be used for evaluating system performance should include recall, precision, average number of stages for retrieving the relevant images, average rank of the relevant images, effectiveness of query language and model, effectiveness of relevance feedback.

12 Speed is not of central concern. While we clearly cannot ignore the speed of retrieval completely, it is primarily the software ability to identify visual information rather than the hardware efficiency that constitutes the main focus.

9. Design Questions

Researchers, students, and practitioners in charge of designing a CBIR system are faced with numerous questions, some of which are summarized next.

- *Which features should be used and how should they be represented?*

  The feature extraction stage is a critical piece of the puzzle. Even though good feature extraction algorithms alone do not guarantee the overall success of a CBIR system, no system will exhibit a good performance if its knowledge about the images' low-level contents is less than the minimum required to establish the notion of visual similarity between images.

- *Which measure of dissimilarity should be used?*

The most widely adopted similarity model is metric and assumes that human similarity perception can be approximated by measuring distances between feature vectors. In our implementation (MUSE), we tested several combinations of features and dissimilarity measures. The results of these experiments are reported in Chapter 6.

- *Which types of queries should be supported?*

  We advocate that a CBIR system should offer at least the following types of access to the visual contents of an image database:

  - Interactive browsing. Users should be able to use a built-in browser to navigate through thumbnails of the images in the repository.
  - Query by example (QBE). Users can open an image file and use it as an example of the image(s) they are searching for. Technical users can also specify which features and distance measurements should be used in the search.

- *How can the system know which features to use or give preference to in a particular query?*

  There are two possible ways of dealing with this issue:

  (a) Let the user explicitly indicate which features are important before submitting the query. This alternative is sometimes offered to the technical user in several CBIR systems working under the QBE paradigm.

  (b) Use machine learning techniques to understand the importance of each (set of) feature(s) based on the users' interactions and relevance feedback.

- *How to evaluate the quality of the results?*

  Due to the lack of established benchmarks for testing CBVIR systems, each developer has been testing their systems with arbitrary image repositories, whose size is normally between 1,500 and 60,000 images and whose diversity is such as to discourage the use of specialized feature extractors.

- *Where will the image files be located?*

  The knowledge about where the image files are actually stored (in a local hard drive or spread over the Internet) makes a big difference in the design of the system. Among the many issues that need to be taken into account when the images are not stored locally, we can mention:

(a) the need to store locally either a thumbnail version or a mirrored copy of each image in the remote database;

(b) the possibility that the actual image files might be (temporarily or permanently) unavailable;

(c) possible performance degradation caused by network congestion;

(d) different strategies to update the indexes according to changes in the image repository.

- *How can the user provide relevance feedback and what should the system do with it?*

  In CBIR systems that support relevance feedback, these are very important issues. The first impacts the design of the user interface and the options available to users to express their opinion about the image used as an example (if the system follows a QBE paradigm), the features used to measure similarity, and the partial results obtained so far.

  The second issue relates to the complex calculations that take into account the user's relevance feedback information and translate it into an adjustment on the query, the importance of each feature, the probability of each image being the target image, or a combination of those.

- *Which supporting tools could be advantageously added to the system?*

  CBIR systems can be enhanced with a set of supporting tools, such as those suggested in [73]. One example of such tool is a collection of basic image processing functions that would allow users of a QBE-based system to do some simple editing (e.g., cropping, color manipulation, blurring or sharpening, darkening or lightening) on the sample image before submitting their query, such as the Mirage set of tools [40], implemented within the context of the MUSE project.

10. Summary

This chapter summarized the main concepts and questions behind the design of CBIR systems. It discussed design choices for the most important building blocks of a CBIR system — from feature extraction to relevance feedback — and gave pointers to representative references in these topics.

Chapter 4

DESIGNING A CONTENT-BASED VIDEO RETRIEVAL SYSTEM

This chapter extends the discussion of the main questions behind the design of content-based image retrieval systems to their video counterparts. It examines the main concepts, algorithms, and challenges in building content-based video indexing, browsing, and retrieval systems.

1. The Problem

The human derivation of textual descriptions from video contents has the same limitations previously described in the discussion of text-based indexing of image data: it is subjective, incomplete, biased, inaccurate, and — even more — time consuming. Many of the principles, ideas, techniques, and algorithms devised for content-based image retrieval can be extended to video retrieval, but such extensions are not as simple as giving to each video frame the same treatment one would give to individual images. Indexing each individual frame as an image would produce a prohibitively high amount of redundant metadata, wasting valuable storage and processing resources. Moreover, because video is a structured medium in which actions and events in time and space convey stories, a video program must be viewed as a document, not a non-structured sequence of frames. Therefore, the video contents have to be decomposed into structural components, and the indexes should be built upon this structural information as well as the contents of individual frames [196].

The challenges behind the design and implementation of content-based video indexing, browsing, and retrieval systems have attracted researchers from many disciplines, ranging from image processing, to databases to speech recognition, to mention just a few. Such a broad range of expertise has been recognized by the research community as necessary to tackle this inherently complex problem. It is widely accepted that successful solutions to the problem of understanding and indexing video data will require a blend of information from different sources, such as speech, sound, text, and images [196].

2. The Solution

The process of building indexes for video programs normally involves three main steps:

1 **Video parsing**: consists of temporal segmentation of the video contents into smaller units. Video parsing techniques extract structural information from the video program by detecting temporal boundaries and identifying meaningful segments, usually called *shots*. The terminology of video parsing and some of the currently used techniques are explained in more detailed in Section 3.

2 **Abstraction**: consists of extracting or building a representative subset of video data from the original video. The most widely used video abstractions are: the *key-frame* (the still image extracted from the video data that best represents the contents of a shot) and the *"highlight" sequence* (a shorter frame sequence extracted from the original shot). The result of the video abstraction stage forms the basis for content-based video representation and browsing. More details about video abstraction are provided in Section 4.

3 **Content analysis**: consists of extracting visual features from representative video frames. Several techniques used for image feature extraction can be used, but they are usually extended to extraction of features that are specific to video sequences, corresponding to the notion of object motion, events, and actions.

The relationships among these stages are illustrated in Figure 4.1.

3. Video Parsing

Similarly to organizing a long text into smaller units, such as paragraphs, sentences, words, and letters, a long video sequence must be organized into smaller and more manageable components, upon which indexes can be built. The process of breaking a video program down into smaller components is known as *video parsing*.

These components are normally organized in a hierarchical way, with five levels, in decreasing degree of granularity: key-frame, shot, group, scene, and video program. The basic structure unit is a *shot*, defined as a sequence of frames recorded contiguously and representing a continuous

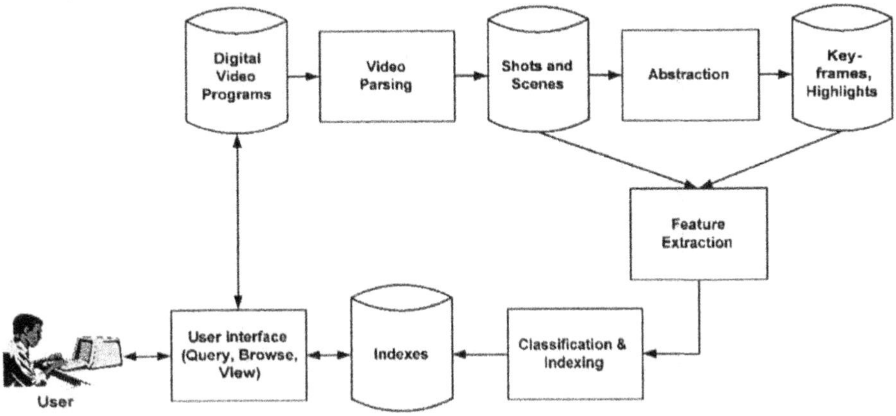

Figure 4.1. Block diagram of a content-based video retrieval system (adapted from [195]).

action in time or space. The most representative frame of a shot is called a *key-frame*. A *scene* or *sequence* is formally defined as a collection of semantically related and temporally adjacent shots, depicting and conveying a high-level concept or story. A video *group* is an intermediate entity between the physical shots and semantic scenes and serves as a bridge between the two. Examples of groups are temporally adjacent shots and visually similar shots [140]. In the following sections we present pointers to a few representative algorithms and techniques for video parsing at a shot level and an overview of the ongoing work on boundary detection at a scene level.

3.1 Shot Boundary Detection

Shot detection is the process of detecting boundaries between two consecutive shots, so that a sequence of frames belonging to a shot will be grouped together [195].

There are different types of boundaries between shots. The simplest one is the *cut*, an abrupt change between the last frame of a shot and the first frame of a subsequent shot. Gradual boundaries are harder to detect. Examples include: dissolves, wipes, fade-ins, and fade-outs. A *fade* is a "gradual means of closing or starting a shot, often used as a transitional device when one scene closes with the image disappearing (a fade-out) and the next scene comes into view as the image grows stronger and stronger (a fade-in) [93]." A *dissolve* is "a transition between two shots whereby the first gradually fades out as the second gradually fades in with some overlap between the two [93]." A wipe is a transition "in which the new shot gradually appears while pushing or 'wiping' off the old [93]." An additional level of difficulty is imposed by camera operations such as panning (the process of moving a camera horizontally around a fixed axis) and zooming (the apparent movement either toward or away from a subject). A robust shot boundary detection algorithm should be able to detect all these different types of boundaries with accuracy.

The basis for detecting shot boundaries is the detection of significant changes in contents on consecutive frames lying on either side of a boundary. Automatic shot boundary detection techniques can be classified into seven main groups:

1 **Pixel-based**

The easiest way to detect a shot boundary is to count the number of pixels that change in value more than some threshold. This total is compared against a second threshold to determine if a shot boundary has been found [20]. The major problems with this approach are its sensitivity to camera movement and noise. Examples of pixel-based shot detection techniques can be found in [76, 77, 122, 194, 198].

2 **Statistics-based**

Statistical methods expand on the idea of pixel differences by breaking the images into regions and comparing statistical measures of the pixels in those regions [20]. For example, Kasturi and Jain [90] use intensity statistics (mean and standard deviation) as shot boundary detection measures. This method is reasonably robust to noise, but slow and prone to generate many false positives (i.e., changes not caused by a shot boundary) [20].

3 **Histogram-based**

The most popular metric for sharp transition detection is the difference between histograms of two consecutive frames. In its simplest form, the gray level or color histograms of two consecutive frames are computed: if the bin-wise difference between the two histograms is above a threshold, a shot boundary is said to be found.

Several variants of the basic idea have been proposed in the literature. Nagasaka and Tanaka [122] proposed breaking the images into 16 regions, using a χ^2-test on color histograms of those regions, and discarding the eight largest differences to reduce the effects of object motion and noise. Swanberg, Shu, and Jain [167] used gray level histogram differences in regions, weighted by how likely the region was to change in the video sequence. Their results were good because their test video (CNN Headline News) had a very regular spatial structure.

Zhang, Kankanhalli, and Smoliar [198] compared pixel differences, statistical differences and several different histogram methods and concluded that the histogram methods were a good trade-off between accuracy and speed. They also noted, however, that the basic algorithm did not perform too well for gradual transitions as it did for abrupt cuts. In order to overcome these limitations, they proposed the *twin-comparison algorithm*, which uses two comparisons: one looks at the difference between consecutive frames to detect sharp cuts, and the other looks at accumulated difference over a sequence of frames to detection gradual transitions. This algorithm also applies a global motion analysis to filter out sequences of frames involving global or large moving objects, which may confuse the gradual transition detection.

Additional examples of histogram-based shot detection techniques include [5, 144, 176, 199, 197].

4 **Transform-based**

Transform-based techniques use the compressed Discrete Cosine Transform (DCT) coefficients present in an MPEG stream as the boundary measure. The first comparison metric based on DCT for partitioning JPEG compressed videos was developed by Arman and colleagues [12] and extended to MPEG by Zhang et al. [197]. In this algorithm, a subset of the blocks in each frame and a subset of the DCT coefficients for each block were used as a vector representation for each frame and the difference metric between frames is defined by content correlation in terms of a normalized inner product between the vector representations of two — not necessarily consecutive — frames.

Yeo and Liu [190] have observed that for detecting shots boundaries, DC components of DCTs of video frames provide sufficient information. Based on the definition of DCT, this is equivalent to a low-resolution version of the frames, averaged over 8x8 non-overlap blocks. This observation has led to yet another method for video segmentation in which, instead of comparing histograms of pixel values, histograms of DCT-DC coefficients of frames are compared.

DCT-based metrics can be directly applied to JPEG video, where every frame is intra-coded. In MPEG, however, DCT-based metrics can be applied only in comparing I-frames. Since only a small portion of frames in MPEG are I-frames, this significantly reduces the amount of processing required to compute differences at the expense of a loss of temporal resolution between I-frames, which typically introduces a large fraction of false positives and requires additional processing [144, 190, 197].

5 **Edge-based**

Zabih, Miller, and Mai [194] proposed an edge-based algorithm that works as follows. Consecutive frames are aligned to reduce the effects of camera motion and the number and position of edges in the edge detected images is recorded. The percentage of edges that enter and exit between the two frames is then computed. Shot boundaries are detected by looking for large edge change percentages. Dissolves and fades are identified by looking at the relative values of the entering and exiting edge percentages. They concluded that their method was more accurate at detecting cuts than histogram-based techniques.

6 **Motion-based**

Zhang, Kankanhalli, and Smoliar [197] used motion vectors determined from block matching to detect whether or not a shot was a zoom or a pan. Shahraray [145] used the motion vectors extracted as part of a region-based pixel difference computation to decide if there is a large amount of camera or object motion in a shot. Because shots with camera motion can be incorrectly classified as gradual transitions, detecting zooms and pans increases the accuracy of a shot boundary detection algorithm. Other examples of motion-based shot detection can be found in [113, 189].

Motion vector information can also be obtained from MPEG compressed video streams. However, the block matching performed as part of MPEG encoding selects vectors based on compression efficiency and thus often selects inappropriate vectors for image processing purposes [20].

7 **Other approaches**

Recent work in shot boundary detection include the use of clustering and postfiltering [123], which achieves reasonably high accuracy without producing many false positives, and the combination of image, audio, and motion information [21].

Several studies [20, 47, 56] have compared shot boundary detection algorithms, and have concluded that histogram-based algorithms and

MPEG compression domain feature-based techniques exhibit the best performance both from accuracy as well as speed vantage points[1].

3.2 Scene Boundary Detection

The automatic detection of *semantic* boundaries (as opposed to *physical* boundaries) within a video program is a much more challenging task and the subject of ongoing research [39, 127, 182]. Part of the problem lies in the fact that scenes and stories are semantic entities that are inherently subjective and lack universal definition or rigid structure. Moreover, there is no obvious direct mapping between these concepts and the raw video contents. Its solution requires a higher level of content analysis.

Two different strategies have been used to solve the problem of automatic scene detection: one based on film production rules, the other based on *a priori* program models. Examples of the former include the work of Aigrain et al. [6] using filming rules (e.g., transition effects, shot repetition, appearance of music in the soundtrack) to detect local (temporal) clues of macroscopic change and the research results of Yeung et al. [191] in which a *time-constrained clustering* approach is proposed, under the rationale that semantically related contents tend to be localized in time. *A priori* model-based algorithms rely on specific structural models for programs whose temporal structures is usually very rigid and predictable, such as news and sports [63, 167, 200].

4. Video Abstraction and Summarization

Video abstraction is the process of extracting a presentation of visual information about the landscape or structure of a video program, in a way that is more economical than, yet representative of, the original video. There are two main approaches to video abstraction: *key-frames* and *"highlight" sequences.*

4.1 Key-frame Extraction

A key-frame is the still image extracted from the video data that best represents the contents of a shot in an abstract manner [196]. The simplest way to extract a key-frame is to use the first, last, and/or middle frame as a key-frame, with no guarantee that the chosen frame will be representative of the semantic contents of the shot. More sophisticated

[1]The reader should note that these studies were published four years ago or earlier and their results should not be interpreted as conclusive. Shot boundary detection is still an active research topic, as indicated by recent papers such as [123].

key-frame extraction techniques are based on visual content complexity indicators [202], shot activity indicators [67], and shot motion indicators [188]. Due to the difficulty in performing true semantic analysis of the contents of the shot to help decide which frame should be selected as a key-frame, many contemporary algorithms [79, 199] rely on low-level image features instead.

4.2 "Highlight" Sequences

This approach — also known as *video skimming* or *video summaries* — aims at abstracting a long video sequence into a much shorter (summary) sequence, with a fair perception of the video contents. A successful approach is to utilize information from multiple sources (e.g., shot boundaries, human faces, camera and object motions, sound, speech, and text). Researchers working on documents with textual transcriptions have suggested producing video abstracts by first abstracting the text using classical text skimming techniques and then looking for the corresponding parts in the video sequence. A successful application of this type of approach has been the Informedia project, in which text and visual content information are merged to identify video sequences that highlight the important contents of the video [159]. The extension of this skimming approach from documentary video programs to other videos with a soundtrack containing more than just speech, remains an open research topic.

5. Video Content Representation, Indexing, and Retrieval

The extraction of content primitives (referred to as "metadata" in the scope of the emerging MPEG-7 standard) from video programs is a required step that allows video shots to be classified, indexed, and subsequently retrieved. Since shots are usually considered the smallest indexing unit in a video database, content representation of video is also usually based on shot features. There are two types of features: those associated with key-frames only — which are static by nature — and those associated with the frame sequence that compose a shot — which may include the representation of temporal variation of any given feature and motion information associated with the shot or some of its constituent objects. Representing shot contents at an object level through the detection and encoding of motion information of dominant objects in the shot is a new and attractive technique, because much of the object information is available in MPEG-4 video streams. Examples of object-based representation of shot contents include [9, 29, 53].

The retrieval of a video clip based on its contents is a much more challenging problem than in image retrieval, because more features, often with different importance, are involved. This is an open and very active research topic [4, 11, 29, 140, 148, 160, 193]. Existing work typically fall within one of these two categories:

- Use content-based image retrieval techniques applied to the key-frames of the video sequences. Although easy to implement, it is limited for lack of temporal information.

- Incorporate motion information (sometimes object tracking) into the retrieval process. Richer queries can be formulated, because now temporal information is available, at the expense of higher computational cost.

6. Video Browsing Schemes

Content-based browsing is another active field of research, aiming at providing the users a convenient way to quickly assess the relevance of a video source material in a friendly, intuitive, and manageable way. The task of browsing is a complement — rather than a replacement — to the retrieval operation. While browsing a collection of video programs can be compared to perusing the table of contents (ToC) of a book, retrieving a video clip based on its contents is equivalent to looking up information in the index [140].

Video browsing tools can be classified in two main types:

- Time-line and light-table display of video frames and/or icons [46, 197]: traditional and straightforward representation, in which video units are organized in chronological sequence.

- Hierarchical or graph-based story board: representation that attempts to present the structure of video in an abstract and summarized manner. Research on content-based browsing has been focusing on this type of browsing. Examples include the work of Zhang et al. on hierarchical browsing [199] and the scene transition graph proposed by Yeung and colleagues [191], later extended to the idea of "video posters" [192].

Tonomura et al. [174] propose several new interfaces for video viewing, including a visualization tool, VideoSpaceIcon, that allows the visualization of temporal and spatial information of a shot combined in a 3D icon. Similar ideas have been reported for video browsing [171, 173, 201].

Video browsing can be performed at two different levels: microscopic and macroscopic. Microscopic browsing refers to browsing at the shot and frame (syntactic unit) levels, while macroscopic browsing refers to high-level browsing at the story and scene (semantic unit) levels. The two forms of browsing complement one another, allowing users to view and navigate video content at different levels of granularity, as well as to focus on a particular level of information abstraction. In microscopic browsing, users want fast, convenient access to individual shots and frames of video and at the same time to conserve the limited bandwidth and network resources available to their systems. Spatially reduced images, such as DC images, can help provide needed browsing capabilities at the frame level. In macroscopic browsing, however, higher-level abstractions of video (visual summaries) (see Section 4) are used to capture the content and structure of the underlying story for intuitive understanding and easy navigation of video.

An ingenious combination of the two approaches, called VideoZoom, was proposed by Smith [153]. VideoZoom allows users to start with coarse, low resolution views of the sequences and selectively zoom in in space and time. VideoZoom decomposes the video sequences into a hierarchy of view elements, which are retrieved in a progressive fashion. The client browser incrementally builds the views by retrieving, caching, and assembling the view elements as needed. By integrating browsing and retrieval into a single progressive retrieval paradigm, VideoZoom is particularly well suited for Internet-based video applications, allowing for content selection without downloading or streaming entire video programs.

7. Examples of Video Retrieval Systems

7.1 VideoQ

Developer. Columbia University, New York

URL. http://ives.ctr.columbia.edu:8888/VideoQ/about.html

References. [29]

Querying. VideoQ is a content-based video search system. It allows the user to search for a particular object, scene, or subject in a large video database. VideoQ provides the user with a wide range of search methods including standard text search based on keywords and content based search based on color, shape, texture, and motion. The visual query is effective when it is combined with text search. The text search is used to pre-filter videos and to reduce the number of videos to be searched using content-based search.

Features. VideoQ automatically extracts coherent visual features such as color, texture, shape, and motion. These features are then grouped into higher semantic knowledge forming video objects and associated

spatio-temporal relationships. VideoQ performs automatic video object segmentation and tracking and also includes query with multiple objects.
Matching. The user typically formulates visual query by sketch. The user can draw objects with a particular shape, paint color and texture, and specify motion. The video objects of the sketch are then matched against those in the database and a ranked list of video shots is returned.
Result Presentation. The retrieved video shots are presented on a separate window, where each shot is identified by a thumbnail version of its key-frame.
Applications. VideoQ is designed to serve as Web-based interactive video engine, where the user queries the system using animated sketches. It includes search and manipulation of MPEG-compressed videos.

7.2 Screening Room

Developer. Convera, Vienna (Virginia)
URL. http://www.convera.com
Platform. Convera offers Screening Room, which is a fully integrated, modular video content management solution. Screening Room provides video capture and analysis, indexing, and video production and publishing of video content to the Internet.
Product Components. Screening Room consists of four components: Video Capture, Video Asset Server, Video Edit, and Video Publish.

- **Video Capture** component provides capturing analog and digital videos including live feeds. It uses video encoding and analysis technology to extract metadata from source material. It then creates an encoded digital proxy, which is a low-resolution copy of the original video as well as a storyboard based on major scene changes, such as cuts, fades, dissolves and time-based events.

- **Video Asset Server** stores the referenced digital video assets, metadata, and indexes created during the capture process. It uses RetrievalWare search engine to search across managed video assets and find and retrieve required video segments.

- **Video Edit** component provides search to quickly locate video, and add, modify and delete metadata and user annotations, review and delete individual storyboard clips of frames, and create new video clips.

- **Video Publish** component provides publishing the selected video, including storyboards, closed captioning and annotations, on the Web.

Customers. Convera's customers include Viacom, Warner Brothers, Johnson Space Center, Discovary Communications, ExTRA BYTES, KABC-TV, World Bank, and others.

7.3 Virage

Developer. Virage, San Mateo (California)

URL. http://www.virage.com

Platform. Virage provides a video product suite that is used for full set of video applications including video production, video capture, indexing and encoding, video publishing and distribution via Internet, and video content delivery and viewing. Virage offers their products either as of-the-shelf software or as application service.

Products. The software products include: VideoLogger, Media Analysis Software, ControlCenter, and Video Application Server.

- VideoLogger performs real time video indexing and creates index database for the incoming video.
- Media Analysis Software includes audio, face and text recognition, which automatically inserts additional tracks of information into the video index.
- ControlCenter remotely controls, centralizes and manages the encoding process for multiple VideoLoggers from one central console.
- Video Application Server is an XML-based application server that allows effective content management.

Customers. Virage's customers include Bloomberg, C-SPAN, CNET, FBI, Library of Congress, Yahoo, EarthLink, AltaVista, ABC News, PBS and others.

8. Summary

As with image retrieval, the complete automation of content-based video browsing and retrieval still depends heavily upon the use of low-level visual features and the research community has agreed that successful solutions will combine different sources of information, such as speech, sound, text, and images in understanding and indexing video data. This is the trend and focus of ongoing research efforts on video content analysis and content-based indexing.

Chapter 5

A SURVEY OF CONTENT-BASED IMAGE RETRIEVAL SYSTEMS

by Remco C. Veltkamp and Mirela Tanase
Department of Computing Science, Utrecht University
Utrecht, The Netherlands
{Remco.Veltkamp,mirela}@cs.uu.nl

1. Introduction

In this chapter we survey some technical aspects of current content-based image retrieval systems.

A number of other overviews on image database systems, image retrieval, or multimedia information systems have been published, see e.g. [49], [54],[69], [70],[72], [89], [135],[170]. The purpose of *this* survey however, is to provide an overview of the functionality of temporary image retrieval systems in terms of technical aspects: querying, relevance feedback, features, matching measures, indexing data structures, and result presentation. It compares specific systems, rather than general architectures, and provides a basis for (or defence against) statements like "this or that system already does what your system does". It also is a thorough foundation for claims that most systems use low level features, and few use high level, semantically meaningful, features.

2. Criteria

Many image retrieval systems can be conceptually described by the framework depicted in figure 5.1. In this chapter we survey how the user can formulate a query, whether and how relevance feedback is possible, what kind of features are used, how features from query image and data base image are matched, how the retrieval results are presented to the user, and what indexing data structures are used.

The user interface typically consists of a query formulation part and a result presentation part. Specification of which images to retrieve from

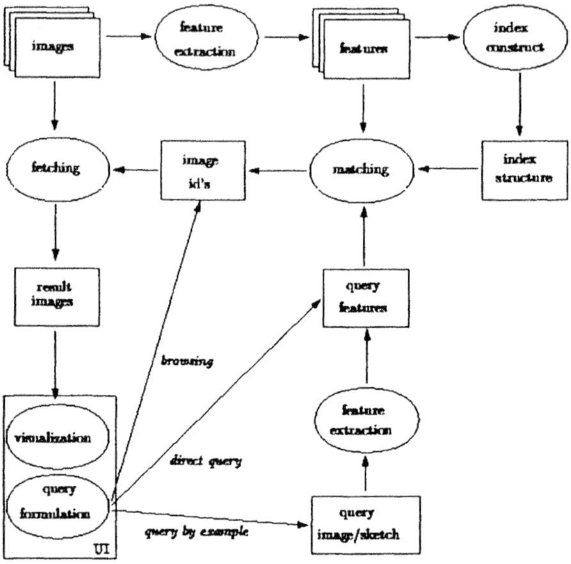

Figure 5.1. Content-based image retrieval framework.

the database can be done in many ways. One way is to browse through the database one by one. Another way is to specify the image in terms of keywords, or in terms of image features that are extracted from the image, such as a color histogram. Yet another way is to provide an image or sketch from which features of the same type must be extracted as for the database images, in order to match these features. A nice taxonomy of interaction models is given in [178]. Relevance feedback is about providing positive or negative feedback about the retrieval result, so that the system can refine the search.

We will consider several classes of features that are used to specify queries: color, texture, shape, spatial layout, and faces. Color features are often easily obtained directly from the pixel intensities, e.g. color histogram over the whole image, over a fixed subimage, or over a segmented region are often used. Although a precise definition of texture is untraceable, the notion of texture generally refers to the presence of a spatial pattern that has some properties of homogeneity. In particular, the homogeneity cannot result from the presence of only a single color in the regions, but requires interaction of various colors.

There is no universal definition of what shape is either. Impressions of shape can be conveyed by color or intensity patterns, or texture, from which a geometrical representation can be derived. In this chapter we consider shape as something geometrical. Therefore, we consider for example edge orientation over all pixels as texture, but edge orientation at only region contours as shape information. Shape descriptors are diverse, e.g. turning angle functions, deformable templates, algebraic moments, and Fourier coefficients. For an overview of shape matching techniques, see [177].

Indexing is often used as identifying features within an image; with indexing data structures we here mean structures to speed up the retrieval of features within image collections.

Spatial layout is about the absolute or relative position of color, texture, or shape information. Higher level features are increasingly more specific, and thus less widely used. However, faces are frequently present in pictures and relatively often used as a feature, so that we tally its use separately.

3. Systems

Below we describe a number of content-based image retrieval systems, in alphabetical order. If no *querying*, *features*, *matching*, *indexing* data structure, or *result presentation* is mentioned, than it is not applicable to the system (e.g. there is no relevance feedback), or no such information is known to us (e.g. often no information is given about indexing data structures).

3.1 ADL (Alexandria Digital Library)

Developer. University of California, Santa Barbara.

URL. The homepage is at `http://www.alexandria.ucsb.edu/adl.html`.

References. [110], [184].

Querying. With a map browser the user can interactively pan and zoom a two-dimensional map of the world to locate his areas of interest, and select a query area that must contain or overlap with the database images. Then, the user can select a catalogue of images, set alphanumeric query parameters such as type (e.g. aerial photos, maps, remote sensing images), and then retrieve the images overlapping with the area indicated with the map browser.

Features. Although it has been reported [108] that images can be searched with texture features, the ADL website does not show this capability. What remains is searching on keywords.

Matching. When the query is sent to the databases, the query area is compared to the object footprints, according to the functioning matching operator ('contains' or 'overlaps'), and those objects that match are potentially members of the result set for the query.

Result presentation. The matched images are shown as thumbnails, and their footprints are shown on the map in the map browser.

Applications. An important focus for ADL's collection is on information supporting basic science, including the Earth and Social Sciences. The image datasets (will) include digital elevation models (DEMs), digital raster graphics (DRGs), scanned aerial photographs, Landsat images, seismic datasets, Sierra Nevada Ecologic Project datasets, and Mojave Ecologic Project datasets.

3.2 AMORE (Advanced Multimedia Oriented Retrieval Engine)

Developer. C & C Research Laboratories NEC USA, Inc.

URL. `http://www.ccrl.com/amore/`.

References. [120], [121].

Features. The image is segmented into at most eight regions of homogeneous color, and downsized to 24×24 pixels. The regions in this picture are directly used for matching [81].

Querying. The user first selects a category of images. An initial set of images can be selected at random or by keyword. Of these images, visually similar images can be retrieved. The query image can also be specified by its URL. In a research version of the system, sketching a query image was possible. The user can indicate the relative importance of color and shape.

Matching. First a correspondence between regions in the query and target image is found. Regions corresponding to the same regions in the other image are merged. The shape similarity between two regions is based on the number of pixels of overlap, a kind of template matching. The color similarity between two regions is the distance in HLS space between the uniform region colors [81].

Indexing. Indexing is performed by the COIR (Content-Oriented Image Retrieval) system, see [83].

Result presentation. The retrieved images are shown as thumbnails, without an explicit order. In a research version of the system, result images were displayed as a scatter plot, with shape and color similarity values at the axes, or on a perspective wall [120].

Applications. AMORE is used in the art retrieval system Arthur (Art Media and Text Hub and Retrieval System, `http://www.isi.edu/cct/arthur/`, developed at the Center for Cultural Technology within the Information Sciences Institute of the University of Southern California.

3.3 ASSERT

Developer. The School of Electrical and Computer Engineering at Purdue University, West Lafayette.

URL. The homepage is at `http://rvl2.ecn.purdue.edu/~cbirdev/WWW/CBIRmain.html`.

References. [149]

Features. A physician delineates a pathology bearing region (PBR) in images. A lobular feature set (LFS) is associated to a lobe or a combination of adjacent lobes. A LFS contains 26 features of PBRs adjacent to the lobular boundary, and 26 features of PBRs interior to it. The features of each PBR include 14 perceptual features that are specific for HRCT lung images, grouped into linear and reticular opacities, nodular opacities, high opacities, and low opacities. In addition, from 255 general purpose features, a sequential forward selection algorithm selected 12: five grey level, five texture, and two shape features. The grey level features are the grey level mean and standard deviation, and bins 6 ,9, and 16 from a 16-bin histogram. The texture features are contrast, entropy, homogeneity, and cluster tendency, all derived from the grey co-occurrence matrix, and the edginess, the ratio of the number edge pixels to the number of pixels in the PBR. The shape features are area, and distance from the PBR region to the enclosing lobular region boundary.

The distribution of the 52-dimensional feature vectors is partitioned into 46 LFS classes.

Querying. A physician delineates a PBR in the query image, from which the features vector is computed.

Matching. The distance between two feature vectors is the Euclidean distance.

Indexing. The 52-dimensional feature space of the LFSs is divided into bins. Each LFS is converted into a hash index by the multi-hash method [68]. The index points to the appropriate bin containing pointers to one or more LFS classes.

Result presentation. The four best matching images are shown.

Applications. Assert is a specifically targeted towards retrieval of high resolution computed tomography images of the lung.

3.4 BDLP (Berkeley Digital Library Project)

Developer. University of California, Berkeley.

URL. The homepage of project is at `http://elib.cs.berkeley.edu/`, a demo of retrieval from all photos in the collection is at `http://elib.cs.berkeley.edu/photos/all.shtml`.

References. [26].

Features. There is a number of alphanumerical keys available for querying: the collection, key words, location, county, and photographer. The colors of each image are quantized into 13 colors bins. Six values are associated with each color bin: the percentage of the image with colors in that bin, and the number of 'very small', 'small', 'medium', 'large', and 'very large' dots of that color found.

Querying. For content-based search, the user can select 13 colors, and indicate the amount ('any', 'partly', 'mostly') of that color in the picture. Also, for colored regions the user can indicate the size ('any', 'small', 'medium', 'large') and the quantity of regions with that color ('any', 'few', 'some', 'many').

Matching. Image features are stored as text strings. For example, a picture of a sky with clouds might have a few large white regions, and a large amount of blue, and would have a feature text string "`mostly_blue large_white_few`". Matching is done by substring matching, e.g. with query string "`large_white%`".

Indexing. All features are put into a relational database (the Informix Universal Server database management system).

Result presentation. The retrieved photos are presented unordered, with id-number, photographer, and collection keys.

Applications. The collections consist of 23195 images of plants, animals, people, and landscapes, 17000 images from the California Department of Water Resources, Corel Stock photos, and aerial photos of the Sacramento river delta region.

3.5 Blobworld

Developer. Computer Science Division, University of California, Berkeley.

URL. `http://elib.cs.berkeley.edu/photos/blobworld/`.

A demo of Blobworld is available at `http://elib.cs.berkeley.edu/photos/blobworld/start.html`.

References. [27].

Features. The features used for querying are the color, texture, location, and shape of regions (blobs) and of the background. The color is described by a histogram of 218 bins of the color coordinates in Lab-space. Texture is represented by mean contrast and anisotropy over the region, as the 2D coordinate $(contrast, contrast \times anisotropy)$. Shape is represented by (approximate) area, eccentricity, and orientation.

Querying. The user first selects a category, which already limits the search space. In an initial image, the user selects a region (blob), and indicates the importance of the blob ('somewhat', 'very'). Next, the user indicates the importance of the blob's color, texture, location, and shape ('not', 'somewhat', 'very'). More than one regions can be used for querying.

Matching. To match two color histograms h_1 and h_2, the quadratic form distance is used: $d(h_1, h_2) = (h_1 - h_2)^T A(h_1 - h_2)$, where $A = (a_{ij})$ is a symmetric matrix of weights representing the similarity between color bins i and j. The distance between two texture descriptors is the Euclidean distance between their coordinates in representation space. The distance between centroids is the Euclidean distance. The distances are combined into a single final distance.

Indexing. Rather than actually computing the distances between the full color histogram vectors of length 218 as $d(h_1, h_2) = (h_1 - h_2)^T A(h_1 - h_2)$, singular value decomposition (SVD) is used to project the histogram vectors onto a lower-dimensional subspace. The resulting points are indexed by an R*-tree [16].

Result presentation. The retrieved images are ranked in linear order, and presented together with the segmented version showing the regions.

Applications. The demo on the web provides retrieval from a collection of 10000 Corel stock photos.

3.6 CANDID (Comparison Algorithm for Navigating Digital Image Databases)

Developer. Computer Research and Applications Group, Los Alamos National Laboratory, USA.

URL. `http://public.lanl.gov/kelly/CANDID/index.shtml`.

References. [92].

Features. Each image is represented by a signature consisting of a weighted sum of Gaussian functions. The color features used are the clusters of spectral bands. The texture features used are the mean, skewness, and kurtosis of each pixel. The feature vectors of all pixels together form a point set in higher-dimensional space. On the basis of the k-means algorithms, clusters are formed. A mean vector and covariance matrix are computed for each cluster, and the associated Gaussian distribution is weighted by the number of elements in the corresponding cluster. The distribution of the feature vectors is now approximated by the weighted sum of the Gaussian distributions.

Querying. The user provides a query image.

Matching. The dissimilarity between two image signatures is based on the normalized Euclidean distance or the inner product of two signatures.

Result presentation. Each pixel is assigned to one cluster, and each associated Gaussian distribution makes some contribution to the dissimilarity measure. In order to show which parts of the images contribute to the match, each pixel is highlighted depending on the contribution made to the similarity measure.

Applications. CANDID is used in the retrieval of pulmonary CT images, and multispectral Landsat satellite images.

3.7 C-bird (Content-Based Image Retrieval from Digital libraries)

Developer. School of Computing Science, Simon Fraser University, Burnaby, B.C., Canada.

URL. `http://jupiter.cs.sfu.ca/cbird/`.

References. [104], [105].

Features. For each collected image, a feature descriptor and a layout descriptor are computed. A feature descriptor is a set of four vectors: a color vector, a most frequent color (MFC) vector, a most frequent orientation (MFO) vector, and a chromaticity vector. A 512-bin RGB histogram is stored in the color vector. The centroids of the regions associated with the 5 most frequent colors form the MFC vector and the centroids of regions of the 5 most frequent edge orientations form the MFO vector. The 36-dimensional chromaticity vector is computed as follows: first, a normalization of each RGB channel is made to obtain illumination invariance, then the 3D color histogram is replaced by a 2D chromaticity histogram. Treating this chromaticity histogram as an image, first a wavelet-based image reduction is applied, then the Discrete Cosine Transform coefficient matrix is built. The chromaticity vector is made of the 36 values of the upper left corner of the DCT matrix. For search by object model, some geometric data such as the area, the centroid and the eccentricity are computed from color regions associated with each of the MFCs.

The layout descriptor contains a color layout vector and an edge layout vector. To construct these vectors the image is divided into 64 cells, and for each cell the most frequent colors and the number of edges for each orientation are determined.

Also, for images at half and quarter resolution, a feature descriptor like the one described above is stored.

Querying. The user is presented a grid of consecutive images from the database starting at a random position. To start a query by color histogram or color similarity with illumination invariance, one of the buttons under the selected query image is pressed. For a query by color or texture layout, grids are presented for drawing color, texture density and edge orientation layout. For a query by color percentage, 5 colors and their percentages are indicated by the user. For a query by object model, the user browses through a selection of query images and makes a choice.

Matching. The distance between two chromaticity vectors in an illumination invariant color query is the L_2 distance. Texture orientation histograms, as well as color histograms for the full image, are matched by histogram intersection.

The first step in a query by object model is a color localization: color regions for each MFC are extracted and for each region, some geometric data such as the area, the centroid and the eccentricity are computed. After selecting the images in the database that share a number of color regions with the query image, a number of vectors are produced by connecting the centroid of the first MFC region with the centroids of the other MFCs. Analyzing the length of these vectors and the angles between them, a hypothesis regarding the existence of an object at a certain scale and orientation (the difference of angles between centroids of the regions corresponding to the MFCs in the query and database image) is made. This hypothesis is tested in a second step by comparing the texture histogram for each pair of matching regions in the two images. The 2D texture histogram measures orientation (the gradient direction of the edge pixels) and edge separation from the grey level image. Finally, if there is sufficient similarity in their texture between the query object and the area in the database image where the supposed similar object was identified, a shape verification based on the Generalized Hough Transform is performed [15].

Result presentation. The user can choose the number of rows and columns of the displayed images grid. By clicking on a thumbnail image the user can see some color and texture characteristics of the image (color percentage and layout, texture layout).

3.8 CBVQ (Content-Based Visual Query)

Developer. Image and Advanced Television Lab, Columbia university, NY.

References. [154].

Features. The first in a series of systems (which include VisualSEEk, SaFE and WebSEEk) developed by the same team at the Columbia University, CBVQ is the only one that enables queries by texture. First, for each pixel in the image a 9-dimensional texture vector is computed. The components of this vector are the magnitudes of the output of a Haar wavelet filter bank with three iterations on the low frequency. Next, by thresholding the output of each filter, 9 binary images are produced, one for each spatial-frequency subband in the wavelet decomposition. The image pixels are merged into regions of homogeneous texture by using non-linear filtering on each binary image to reduce the noise in the texture content, followed by a sequential labeling algorithm and then a reconstruction of the image by overlapping regions from the binary subband images. Each region is represented by a 9-dimensional binary vector, where each 1 represents a high level of spatial-frequency energy within a particular subband. For each texture region detected, spatial information is also extracted, including region centroid, area, and the dimensions of the minimum bounding rectangle. For each database image, a global color histogram is also computed, and a color segmentation of the image is performed (see VisualSEEk).

Querying. The system allows queries by example (the user can select one of the displayed random images or gives the URL address of any image on the Web) and direct queries (by constructing a color histogram). After selecting the query image in a query by example, the user chooses one of the available search methods: color histogram, color composition, texture and histogram manipulation (the query image histogram can be used to construct a new query histogram).

Matching. Matching by texture regions is most probably done in the same way as color region matching is performed in VisualSEEk.

Indexing. See VisualSEEk.

Result presentation. The best 20 matches are presented to the user in decreasing similarity order, together with the matching score.

Relevance feedback. Any of the retrieved images can be chosen as the new query image.

3.9 Chabot

Developer. Department of Computer Science, University of California, Berkeley, CA, USA.

URL. `http://http.cs.berkeley.edu/~ginger/chabot.html`.

References. [126].

Features. One of the early systems, Chabot aimed at combining text based descriptions with image analysis in retrieving images from a collection of photographs of the California Department of Water Resources. The system made use of an existing text description database of the collection, adding other types of textual information for querying such as the shooting date, the picture location, the perspective of the photo. For each image a color histogram containing only 20 bins is computed.

Querying. The user is presented with a list of search criteria (such as keywords, photographer, film format, shooting date, perspective, location, and colors). The color criterion offers limited options for the user to choose from, such as 'mostly red' or 'some yellow'. The user has the possibility to define concepts, which are combinations of search criteria that the concept satisfies. For example, the concept of 'sunset' is defined as a a combination of keyword ('sunset') and color ('mostly red' or 'mostly orange') criteria.

Matching. To match a 'mostly ...' color criterion, more than 50% of the pixels in an image must have the requested color. For the 'some ...' color criterion, one or two of the 20 colors in the histogram must be qualified as the requested color.

Indexing. The images and associated data are stored in the database POSTGRES, developed at the University of California, Berkeley.

Result presentation. Images are shown without specific order.

Applications. The database contains 11643 images of California natural resources.

3.10 CHROMA (Colour Hierarchical Representation Oriented Management Architecture)

Developer. School of Computing, Engineering and Technology, University of Sunderland, UK.

URL. `http://osiris.sund.ac.uk/~cs0sla/`.

References. [99]

Features. From each image a color dominance vector is generated, of at most length ten. The vector lists the color classes of decreasing dominance. There are ten classes: {uncertain colors like very dark and very bright}, {white}, {grey}, {black}, {red, pink}, {brown, dark yellow, olive}, {yellow, orange, light yellow}, {green, line}, {blue, cyan, aqua, turqoise}, {purple, violet, magenta}. Each pixel of an image tallies for one class, the first vector component is the class with the highest count, etc. If a class does not occur in the image, the vector does not contain this class, and has less than ten components.

A second feature is a 15×15 matrix of color classes. First the image is represented at 15×15 resolution, which color quantization algorithm is used is not mentioned. The matrix contains the color class of each pixel. This provides a rough description of layout in the image.

Querying. The user can navigate through a hierarchy, built on the color dominance vectors of all images in the database. The root contains all images. Each branch i below the root contains all images whose color dominance vector starts with i. Each branch j below each node i contains all images whose vector starts with ij, etc. The user can temporarily omit selected color groups.

A second way of querying is with a sketch or query image, whose 15×15 matrix is matched with the database images' matrices.

Matching. The matching score of two images is the Jaccard's coefficient of their matrices, which is the number of matrix elements that are equal, divided by the maximum number, 225.

Indexing. Except for the navigation, no indexing data structure is used. The querying with an image or sketch involves matching all database images.

Result presentation. The resulting images are presented in linear order of matching score.

3.11 DrawSearch

Developer. Department of Electrical and Electronic Engineering, Technical University of Bari, Italy.

References. [52].

Features. The features used for querying are color, texture and shape. The image is divided into 4×4 subimages and within each subimage, the average color is computed. This results in a 48-length color vector. Shape is represented by means of Fourier descriptors. It is unclear how the contour-based segmentation of the image is done. The components of the shape descriptor are the real part of the lower 100 Fourier coefficients. Texture-based image segmentation makes use of Gaussian Markovian Random Fields.

Querying. The system has two user interfaces: one that allows queries by color and shape, and the other one allowing queries by texture. In the first subsystem, the user draws a sketch on a canvas, selecting color attributes for the lines and closed regions. In the texture retrieval subsystem, a query is posed by selecting a texture area within a database image.

Matching. In the color/shape subsystem, the similarity between two feature vectors is given by the cosine metric. The similarity score between a query and a database image is calculated as a weighted sum of the distances between the two color vectors and shape descriptors.

Result presentation. Images are displayed in decreasing similarity order.

Relevance feedback. In the retrieval by texture subsystem, the user can improve retrieval results by selecting relevant images from the displayed query results. The other subsystem allows both relevant and nonrelevant images to be marked by the user when reiterating the query. The new query vector is computed by combining the feature vector of the original query Q with the feature vectors of relevant and nonrelevant images: $Q^{k+1} = Q^k + \delta \sum_{i=1}^{n_{rel}} X_i - \epsilon \sum_{j=1}^{n_{notrel}} Y_j$, where δ, ϵ are positive real weights, X_i is the feature vector of the ith relevant image, and Y_j of the jth nonrelevant image.

3.12 FIDS (Flexible Image Database System)

Developer. Department of Computer Science and Engineering, University of Washington, Seattle, WA, USA.

URL. `http://www.cs.washington.edu/research/imagedatabase/`.

References. [19].

Features. FIDS uses the following features. The color histogram, and the fraction of flesh colored pixels. The histogram of values after applying the Sobel edge filter. The local binary pattern histogram. The coefficients of the Haar wavelet decomposition. These features are also taken of subimages in a grid, in rows, and columns.

Querying. The user chooses an image as query image. He can select the feature distance measures, and combine them into an overall distance measure. A result image can be used as next query image.

Matching. The distances between the histograms are the L_1-distance. The distance between wavelet coefficients, is some weighted difference. An overall distance can be composed by taking the weighted sum, maximum, or minimum of the individual feature distances, which preserves metric properties.

Indexing. In a preprocessing step, the distance of all database objects to m reference objects are computed, and stored in a so-called trie structure [58]. At query time, the distances d_i, $i = 1, \ldots, m$ of the query to these reference objects are also computed. These both distances and the triangle inequality are used to establish a lower bound on the distance between the query and the database images. The trie structure is used to filter the database images on this lower bound.

Result presentation. The images can be ordered on their lower bound, so that no exact distances between query and images need to be calculated. Alternatively, the user can select of how many of those the true distance must be calculated.

3.13 FIR (Formula Image Retrieval)

Developer. Developed by Fraunhofer Institute for Computer Graphics, Darmstadt, Germany, in association with TXT Ingegneria Informatica S.P.A. (Italy), Giunti Multimedia Srl (Italy), Epsilon Software (Greece), and Kino TV & Movie Productions S.A. (Greece), as part of the Esprit IV project FORMULA.

URL. http://www.igd.fhg.de/igd-a7/projects/formula/formula_e.html.

References. [181].

Features. Basic shape and color information of an image are represented using a multiresolution wavelet decomposition. A preprocessing step include a rescaling of the image to a square thumbnail of 128×128 pixels and a transformation of the thumbnail colors from the RGB space to CIELUV space. Next, a non-standard two-dimensional Haar wavelet transform is performed on each color channel individually, followed by a truncation of the resulting coefficients. Only the coefficients larger than a threshold are retained and after rounding to integer values they are stored in a feature vector.

Querying. A query is submitted by giving an example image.

Matching. The distance measure between two feature vectors is a weighted Euclidean distance, with different weights for each of the resolution levels in the wavelet decomposition.

3.14 FOCUS (Fast Object Color-based Query System)

Developer. Department of Computer Science, University of Massachusetts, Amherst, MA.

URL. http://wagga.cs.umass.edu/~mdas/color_proj.html.

A demo of the system is available at http://cowarie.cs.umass.edu/~colordemo/mdas/demo1/phase0.html.

References. [48].

Querying. The user can select as query one of the displayed template images, or create a new template by marking a subimage which contains the region of interest.

Features. Each image is divided in cells of 100×100 pixels and for each cell a color histogram in the HSV space, coarsely quantized along the saturation and value axes ($64 \times 10 \times 10$), is computed. The peaks of all local histograms are determined and combined in a list of unique peaks for the whole image by merging multiple copies of the same peak. Also, a frequency table is constructed which, for each color in the HSV space, gives the number of images that have a peak of that color.

The spatial relationships between color regions are represented by means of a spatial proximity graph (SPG) constructed in two phases. First an intermediate SPG is generated, with one node corresponding to each color peak computed for the image cells. Two nodes in this graph are connected if their corresponding peaks are located in the same cell or are located in neighboring cells and have the same color. This graph is then simplified, by unifying all connected nodes of the same color in a single node, and stored using an adjacency matrix representation.

For the query image, a global color histogram is computed and color region relationships are determined at pixel level.

Matching. The peaks of a query image are subjected to approximate range queries in the increasing order of their corresponding entries in the frequency table. From the resulting lists, the set of images which have peaks matching all query peaks are determined. For the images in this set, a matching score is computed as the the sum of the L_1 distances between each query peak and the matched candidate peak.

To match the SPG of the query image with that of a candidate image, first the candidate SPG is reduced by removing any node whose corresponding peak does not match a query peak. Then it is checked if the query graph appears as a subgraph in the candidate SPG.

Indexing. The color peaks of the database images are stored in a B^+ tree [94] sorted with hue as the primary key, followed by saturation and value.

Result presentation. When the user submits a query by clicking on an image, the images are retrieved using the first phase of matching (the images displayed are the images that have all the colors of the query image). By clicking on the 'Refine Results' button, the retrieved images are subjected to the second phase of matching, where the spatial relationships of the matched color regions is analyzed in order to detect a query object in a candidate image.

Applications. The database consists of 400 advertisements and 800 color natural images.

3.15 ImageRETRO (Image RETrieval by Reduction and Overview)

Developer. Department of Computer Science, University of Amsterdam, The Netherlands.

URL. `http://carol.wins.uva.nl/~vendrig/imageretro/`.

For a demo of the system, look at `http://python.wins.uva.nl:6022/`.

References. [179].

Querying. The user is shown a number of images (called overview), each of them being representative for a part of the image collection. By selecting one of these images, the user selects a part of the database, which is then clustered, and another set of representative images is shown to the user. By this successive filtering, the user obtains a small set of images which can be browsed manually.

Features. The following features are used in clustering images: *a 15-bin hue histogram*, *the number of colors* (the number of bins with more pixels than a threshold, relative to the total number of bins in the hue histogram), *the average color* (the center of gravity of the circular hue histogram is the bin which gives the lowest average value when taken as a starting point in computing this value; the average value is given by $avg = (\sum_{j=1}^{15} h_j d_j)/h$, where h_j represents the number of pixels in bin j, d_j is the distance from this bin to the starting point in the circular hue histogram, and $h = \sum_{j=1}^{15} h_j$; the average color is the average value of the center of gravity divided by 15), *the color variation* (the circular hue histogram is first linearized by using the center of gravity as the center of the new histogram; the standard deviation of this histogram normalized by the maximal possible standard deviation gives the color variation), *the grayness* (share of gray valued pixels in the total number of pixels), *the average gray value* (average value of the gray value histogram, see average color), *the average saturation* (the sum of saturation values for each pixel divided by the total number of pixels), *the background proportion* (share of the background in the total number of pixels, where the supposed background is the bin with the highest frequency in the hue or the gray value histogram), *the number of regions* (a region is a collection of adjacent pixels with the same color hue or gray value), *the number of holes* (relative to the number of regions, where a hole is a region surrounded entirely by another region). For all the images in the database, the color features described above are computed off-line and stored in the database.

Matching. The ranking of the image clusters, employed in the relevance feedback, is straightforward when based on one of the scalar color features. No histogram distance measure is mentioned.

Relevance feedback. Let I_s be the image set after s reductions (filterings) and let F denote the set of 10 color features described. The image set is clustered based on an automatically selected feature subset F_s of F. The images from I_s are ranked independently for each feature in F_s, and each such ranking is divided into 4 clusters (corresponding to a reduction of 25%) and each cluster centroid is chosen as the cluster representative. The union of these representatives for all rankings forms the representative set of I_s, which will be shown to the user for the next reduction. The choice of feature subset F_s at stage s in the retrieval process is based on statistical analysis. For each feature, the variance of the feature values of all images is computed and F_s is made of the features with highest variances, that do not highly correlate with each other.

Applications. The system was tested with a database of 10000 images, collected from the Web.

3.16 ImageRover

Developer. Department of Computer Science, Boston University, MA.

URL. `http://www.cs.bu.edu/groups/ivc/ImageRover/`.

For a demo of the system, look at `http://www.cs.bu.edu/groups/ivc/ImageRover/demo.html`.

References. [142], [172].

Features. The features used for querying are color and texture orientation. The system computes distributions of color and orientation over 6 subimages (the whole image and 5 subregions: the central and corner regions). The result is an image index vector made of 2×6 subvectors. This dimension is subject to a reduction via a principal component analysis (PCA) for each of the subvector spaces. Image color histograms are computed in the CIELUV color space and each histogram quantizes the color space into 64 bins. The texture direction distribution is calculated using steerable pyramids. At each of the four levels of the pyramid, texture direction and strength for each pixel is calculated resulting in an orientation histogram, quantized to 16 bins.

Querying. The user starts a query session by specifying a set of keywords related to the desired images. From the set of images displayed, the user finds and marks one or more images which are similar to what she/he is looking for. Apart from selecting relevant images, the user can deselect one or more of the query images before reiterating a new query. There is no limit to the number of iterations in providing relevance feedback, nor in the number of example images.

Matching. Based on relevance feedback from the user, the system selects the appropriate $\tilde{L}_m$ normalized Minkowski metric each time a query is made. The normalization factor μ^i_m, employed by the normalized distance $\tilde{L}_m(x_i, y_i) = L_m(x_i, y_i)/\mu^i_m$, with x_i and y_i being two subvectors of the image index vectors X and Y, is the expected value over the entire database: $\mu^i_m = E[\tilde{L}_m(x_i, y_i)]$. It is allowed to use metrics of different orders m_i for each of the image index subvectors. Thus, if S is a set of relevant images indicated by the user, the appropriate value for m of the i-th subvector is chosen so as to minimize the distance between relevant images: $m_i = arg\ \min_m E[\tilde{L}_m(p_i, q_i)]$, over all $P, Q \in S$.

Then the k-nearest neighbor search of the image index vector uses the following weighted distance metric:

$d(X,Y) = (w_1, \ldots, w_n)(\tilde{L}_{m_1}(x_1, y_1), \ldots, \tilde{L}_{m_n}(x_n, y_n))^T$
where X, Y are the image index vectors and w_i are relevance weights.

Indexing. An optimized kD tree is used and the search algorithm in this structure employs an approximation factor. The user can select through the search accuracy button one of the three values for this approximation factor.

Result presentation. Images similar to the query images are shown in decreasing similarity order. Their number is chosen by the user. Each displayed thumbnail image is a hypertext link to the original image, allowing the user to retrieve the desired image from its home website.

Relevance feedback. The user indicates the more relevant images, after which the system selects the appropriate $\tilde{L}_m$, see above.

Applications. Image Rover is an image search engine for the WWW.

3.17 ImageScape

Developer. Department of Computer Science, Leiden University, The Netherlands.

URL. `http://www.wi.leidenuniv.nl/home/lim/image.scape.html`.
A demo is available at `http://ind134a.wi.leidenuniv.nl:2001/new2/imagesearch.demo.html`.

References. [24], [102].

Querying. Using the sketch interface, the user can draw an outline of the desired image. For semantic querying, the user brings icons on a canvas that represent the objects/concepts he is looking for, at the desired position in the image. Examples of object/concept categories include human faces, stone or sand, water, sky, tree or grass, points and lines.

Features. Edge maps of the images collected by Web crawlers are obtained using the Sobel operator and a Gaussian blurring filter. A frequency histogram of the 3×3 binary pixel patterns occurring in the edge image, which is called trigram vector, is computed for all images. This vector is subjected to a dimensionality reduction using a band-pass filter (see LCPD below). Various other features, used in object matching, are taken at pixel level: color, Laplacian, gradient magnitude, local binary patterns, invariant moments and Fourier descriptors.

Matching. The first step of the object matching process uses the L_1 distance on the trigram vectors to retrieve the top 1% matches from the entire database. Among these, 20 matches are selected in a second step, a 20×20 template matching, using the most informative pixels to minimize the misdetection rate. These pixels are found as follows. For each object, a large set of positive and negative examples are used in finding the set of 256 pixels with the greatest discriminatory power, by maximizing the Kullback relative information combined with a Markov random field.

3.18 JACOB (Just A COntent Based query system for video databases)

Developer. Computer Science & Artificial Intelligence Lab, University of Palermo, Italy.

URL. `http://www.csai.unipa.it:80/research/projects/jacob/`.

A demo is available at `http://www.csai.unipa.it:80/research/projects/jacob/jacob_demos.html`.

References. [97].

Features. The system makes queries based on color and texture features. Color is represented by means of a histogram in the RGB space. Texture features used are two measures extracted from the grey-level co-occurrence matrix, the maximum probability $max_{m,n} f(m,n,r,\theta)$, and the uniformity $\sum_m \sum_n (f(m,n,r,\theta))^2$. An 8-dimensional vector is obtained by computing the joint probability $f(m,n,r,\theta)$ for distance $r = 1$ and orientation $\theta = -45°, 0°, 45°$, and $90°$. Another vector is composed of edge density measures (the fraction of edge pixels in the total number of pixels in the image) along four directions, $-45°, 0°, 45°$, and $90°$.

Querying. The queries may be direct or by example. A direct query is made by inserting a few values representing the color histogram and/or the texture features. For a query by example, the user must give an image.

Matching. Two color histograms H_1, H_2 are compared using the following distance measure: $d(H_1, H_2) = \sum_{y \in S} \sum_{x \in I(y)} |H_1(y) - H_2(x)| s(y, x)$, where S is the reduced RGB space, $I(y)$ is a small interval centered on the point y and s is a color similarity function. The distance measure used for the texture feature vectors is not mentioned. When performing a query, the user choose a value between 0 and 1 to indicate the relative importance of a feature with respect to the other one. As a result the two distances computed are weighted in a global similarity measure.

Result presentation. The system returns the best matching frames in a similarity order. The number of returned frames is chosen by the user.

Applications. The matching of images is used for querying video databases.

3.19 LCPD (Leiden 19th Century Portrait Database)

Developer. Department of Computer Science, Leiden University, The Netherlands.

URL. `http://ind156b.wi.leidenuniv.nl:2000/`.

References. [103].

Features. The user has several choices in selecting the feature vector, the pixel value domain used for computing this vector, and the resolution level. There are three options for the pixel domain: the intensity image, the gradient image (obtained by Sobel operators) and the thresholded gradient image. One feature vector is the horizontal/vertical projection vector. For an image with $m \times n$ pixels, this vector has $m + n$ components computed as the average of the row/column pixel values in the selected space. A second feature is the trigram vector, a frequency histogram of the 3×3 binary pixels patterns in the thresholded gradient image. This 512-length vector can be subjected to a dimensionality reduction and to a component weighting scheme (low weights are applied on either end of the sorted frequency range). A way of reducing the length of the trigram vector is by forming groups of rotation, mirroring and/or intensity invariant binary patterns. By using the RM (Rotation, Mirroring) group, the dimension of the feature vector is reduced to 102 and by forming RIM (Rotation, Intensity, Mirroring) groups to 51. Another method used consists of suppressing the contribution of the black and white patterns (which are among the most common patterns) and the rare patterns. This is called a bandpass filter. A Karhunen-Loeve Transform can also be used for feature vector length reduction.

A similar vector can be constructed in the intensity space. In this case, the feature vector is computed by first thresholding the 8 neighbors of each pixel with its intensity value and counting the number of occurrences of each of the 2^7 possible patterns of these 8 pixels (the center pixel is not part of the pattern). This results in an 256-length local binary pattern vector (LBP), which can also be subjected to dimensionality reduction.

Querying. Querying is done by example. The user first selects a search method (different combinations of pixel domain, feature vector, dimensionality reduction scheme employed and resolution) from the displayed list.

Matching. The similarity between two feature vectors (projections, trigram or LBP vectors) is given by the L_1 distance. If two images have different sizes, the similarity score between two projection vectors is given by the minimum L_1 distance over all possible x-/y-translations of one image over the other. Another similarity measure is given by the magnitude of the the average pixel to pixel difference in the intensity or gradient space.

Indexing. The POSTGRES database stores for each image the best matches for 30 search methods.

Result presentation. Retrieved images are presented in decreasing similarity order.

Applications. The system is used to find near copies of Dutch *carte de visite* studio portraits from a database of 16505 images of photographs taken from 1860 till 1914.

3.20 MARS (Multimedia Analysis and Retrieval System)

Developer. Department of Computer Science, University of Illinois at Urbana-Champaign, further developed at Department of Information and Computer Science, University of California at Irvine, CA.

URL. `http://www-db.ics.uci.edu/pages/research/mars.shtml`.

Demos are available at: `http://www-db.ics.uci.edu/pages/demos/index.shtml`.

References. [129].

Features. The system supports queries on combinations of low-level features (color, texture, shape) and textual descriptions. Color is represented using a 2D histogram over the HS coordinates of the HSV space. Texture is represented by two histograms, one measuring the coarseness and the other one the directionality of the image, and one scalar defining the contrast. In order to extract the color/texture layout, the image is divided into 5×5 subimages. For each subimage a color histogram is computed. For the texture of a subimage, a vector based on wavelet coefficients is used. The object in an image is segmented out in two phases. First, a k-means clustering method in the color-texture space is applied, then the regions detected are grouped by an attraction based method. This consists of choosing a number of attractor regions and associating each region with the attractor that has the largest attraction to it. The attraction between two regions, i and j, is defined as $F_{ij} = M_i M_j / d_{ij}^2$, where M_i, M_j are the sizes of the two regions and d_{ij} is the Euclidean distance between the two regions in the spatial-color-texture space. In the MARS system, five attractors are used: one for each corner of the image (background attractors) and one in the center of the image (the objects attractor). This is consistent with the fact that their database consists of images of single objects. The shape of the boundary of the extracted object is represented by means of Fourier Descriptors (FD).

Querying. Complex queries can be formulated using boolean operators. The desired features can be specified either by example (pointing an image database that has such a property) or direct (for example, by choosing colors from a palette or textures from an available set of patterns).

Matching. The similarity distance between two color histograms is computed by histogram intersection. The similarity between two textures of the whole image is determined by a weighted sum of the Euclidean distance between contrasts and the histogram intersection distances of the other two components, after a normalization of the three similarities. For computing the texture similarity between two corresponding subimages, the Euclidean distance between the vector representations is used. A weighted sum of the 5×5 color/texture similarities is used to compute the color/texture layout distance between two images. The similarity measure between two FD shape representations is a weighted sum of the standard deviations of $ratio(k) = M_2(k)/M_1(k)$ and $shift(k) = \theta_2(k) - \theta_1(k) - \psi$, $k = -N_c, \ldots, N_c$, where $M_i(k)$ and $\theta_i(k)$ are the magnitude and the phase angle of the FD coefficients, ψ is the difference of the major axis orientations of the two shapes and N_c is the number of FD coefficients.

Each query has a query tree associated. In a query tree, the leaves represent the feature vectors (the terms of the boolean expression defining the query) while the internal nodes correspond to boolean operators or more complex terms indicating a query by object. Individual queries on each of the query terms are made. The tree is evaluated bottom-up: each internal node receives from each child a list of ranked images and combines these lists, after a normalization process, according to the weights on the parent-child links.

Indexing. There is no information about indexing data structures used for queries. A new version of the system, WebMARS, is developed where the feature vectors are indexed using hybrid trees, which combine aspects of several indexing trees.

Result presentation. Images are listed in order of decreasing similarity.

Relevance feedback. Initially, the weights of the edges in the query tree are equal for the children of the same parent and their sum is 1. Based on the relevant images chosen by the user from the query result list, a tree reweighting process takes place.

Applications. The database consists of images of ancient African artifacts from the Fowler Museum of Cultural History at UCLA.

3.21 MetaSEEk

Developer. Image and Advanced Television Lab, Columbia University, NY, USA.

URL. `http://www.ctr.columbia.edu/metaseek/`.

References. [17].

Features. Content-based retrieval can be done on the basis of color and texture. MetaSEEk has a color or texture matching and indexing of its own to cluster query images in a local performance database, used to select target search engines. The actual image matching is forwarded to QBIC, VIR Image Engine, WebSEEk, and the VisualSEEk retrieval engines.

Querying. The user can select a category, provide a key word, provide a URL of an image, or select a shown image. Upon receiving a query, the dispatcher consults the performance database at the MetaSEEk site. This database contains performance scores of past query successes and failures of each supported search option. This is used to select the target search engines to be queried.

Indexing. Query images in the performance database are clustered into several classes on the basis of color, textures, and the combination of both. When the user issues a query with a new image for which no performance scores are available, the system downloads the image, and matches it to the corresponding clusters in order to obtain a list of the most similar clusters. Selected images from the few closest clusters are presented to the user, who can choose one. In this way, new queries are related to the performance of past ones for which performance information is available.

Matching. Color and texture are extracted locally by MetaSEEk for the clustering. Color similarity is computed by calculating the color histogram of an image. Texture is computed by measuring the coarseness, contrast, and presence/absence of directionality of an image. The distance between two feature vectors is the Euclidean distance.

Result presentation. The display component merges and ranks the results form each search option.

Relevance feedback. The user can indicate to like or dislike each of the returned images. This information is used to modify the corresponding entries in the performance database.

3.22 MIR (Multimodal Information Retrieval System)

Developer. Center of Excellence for Document Analysis and Recognition, University at Buffalo, NY, USA.

URL. `http://www.cedar.buffalo.edu/MMIR/`.

A demo of the system is available at `http://www.cedar.Buffalo.EDU/MMIR/demo/index.html`.

References. [161], [162].

Features. The MIR system combines various techniques from text processing and image processing in an attempt to derive semantic descriptions of images. By employing natural language processing (NLP) techniques in analyzing image captions, information about the picture's content is derived. This includes whether there are people in the picture, their names, location and time of the photograph, spatial relationships of the people in the image as well as other visual characteristics (attributes that can assist in face recognition such as gender, hair color, beards, mustaches and glasses). Also, statistical text indexing techniques are used in capturing the general context of the image (such as indoor versus outdoor). The pictures in which the presence of people is detected by NLP, are subjected to a face detection to verify this hypothesis. The face detection algorithm uses a three-contour model representing hair line, and left and right outlines of the face. After extracting edges at different image resolutions by means of a wavelet transform, a graph-matching generates possible face candidates in the image. After the face detection, the face areas are cropped out, and for the rest of the image a color histogram is computed. For the scenery pictures (where no face is detected in the NLP analysis) a color correlation histogram is computed. If $\{i, j, k\}$ is a color triple in the $2 \times 2 \times 2$ quantized HVS space, then h^l_{ijk} denotes the number of occurrences of three pixels of these colors as the vertices of a isosceles right triangle with the smaller sides of length l. The color correlation histogram f^l_{ijk} is $h^l_{ijk}/(4 * h_i)$, where h_i is the ith bin of the traditional color histogram.

Querying. A query formulation can include a text string, an image, and a topic (selected from a predefined set containing sports, politics, entertainment etc.). The user can also indicate the relative importance of text versus image content, as well as of background versus foreground in an image containing people (the foreground).

Matching. The similarity between a query and a database image is a weighted sum of the similarities between different sources of information (text-based and content-based) extracted from the image. Two color correlation histograms are matched using the Euclidean distance.

Applications. The system retrieves pictures of people and/or similar scenery in various contexts. Three databases were used in testing the system. The first one consisted of approximately 5000 images with accompanying text provided by United Press International. The second one provided by Kodak consists of consumer photos accompanied by speech annotations. The third one consists of multimodal documents downloaded from the Web.

3.23 NETRA

Developer. Department of Electrical and Computer Engineering, University of California, Santa Barbara, CA.

URL. `http://maya.ece.ucsb.edu/Netra/`.

A demo of the system is available at `http://maya.ece.ucsb.edu/Netra/netra.html`.

References. [107], [108].

Features. Images in the database are segmented into regions of homogeneous color. Of those regions, the following features are extracted: color, texture, shape, and spatial location.

On the basis of a training set of images, the RGB color space is quantized, and represented by a color codebook of 256 colors, the centroids of the quantization cells. The colors of an image region are also quantized, giving a color feature vector $f_c = (c_0, p_0, \ldots, c_n, p_n)$, with c_i the index into the color code book, and p_i the fraction of that color in the region, $p_0 + \ldots + p_n = 1$. The number n is the number of colors used to represent the region, which is different for each region.

Texture is represented by a feature vector f_t containing the normalized mean and standard deviation of a series of Gabor wavelet transforms of the image: $f_t = (\mu_{0,0}, \ldots, \mu_{s,k}, \sigma_{0,0}, \ldots, \sigma_{s,k})$, with s the number of scales, and k the number of directions.

There are three feature vectors used to represent the shape of regions. The first, f_K, is based on the curvature function of the contour, giving the curvature at each point on the contour. The second, f_R is based on the centroid distance function, giving at each contour point the distance to the centroid of the region. The third, f_Z, is the complex coordinate function, representing each contour point as a complex number with real component equal to the x-coordinate, and the imaginary component equal to the y-coordinate. On 64 samples of each of these functions, the fast Fourier transform (FFT) is applied, of which the real (amplitude) component of the coefficients is used, the numbers $F_{-31}, \ldots, F_{32}$. The feature vectors are as follows: $f_K = (|F_1|, \ldots, |F_{32}|)$, $f_R = (|F_1|, \ldots, |F32|)/|F_0|$, $f_Z = (|F_{-31}|, \ldots, |F_{-1}|, |F_2|, \ldots, |F_{32}|)/|F_1|$.

Querying. There are 2,500 images from the Corel photo collection, organized in 25 categories, with 100 images in each category. You can select any one of them as the query image. All images in the database have been segmented into homogeneous regions. You can click on one of the regions and select one of the four image attribute color, spatial location, texture, and shape. Instead of using an image example, you can also directly specify the color and spatial location. The spatial location querying tool utilizes two bounding boxes to define the area of interest. The inner box is used to define the preferred area, and the box outside is used to constrain the objects to be within this area. Thus, if the object has any its bodies exceeding this outside box, they will not be considered.

Matching. Consider two color feature vectors, f_c^A of region A, and f_c^B of region B. For each color c_i in f_c^A, the closest color c_k^B in f_c^B is found, and the distance $d(c_i^A, f_c^B)$ is calculated as the weighted Euclidean distance in RGB space: $d(c_i^A, f_c^B) = |p_i^A - p_k^B| d(c_i^A, c_k^B)$. The distance between the two color feature vectors is now $\sum_{i=0}^{n^A} d(c_i^A, f_c^B)$ + $\sum_{i=0}^{n^B} d(c_i^B, f_c^A)$. The distance between two texture feature vectors is the L_1-distance. The distance between two shape feature vectors is the Euclidean distance.

Indexing is based on the SS-tree [186]. Color, texture, and shape are indexed separately. The first feature the user specifies is used to retrieve about 100 candidates. Then this feature and the possible other features together are used to order the retrieval result.

Result presentation. The matched images are linearly ordered.

Applications. An initial prototype of NETRA is used in ADL (see above) to search on texture.

3.24 Photobook

Developer. Vision and Modeling Group, MIT Media Laboratory, Cambridge, MA.

URL. `http://vismod.www.media.mit.edu/vismod/demos/photobook/index.html`.

References. [132].

Features. Photobook implements three different approaches to constructing image representations for querying purposes, each for a specific type of image content: faces, 2D shapes and texture images. The first two representations are similar in the way that they offer a description relative to an average of a few prototypes by using the eigenvectors of a covariance matrix as an orthogonal coordinate system of the image space. First a preprocessing step is done in order to normalize the input

image for position, scale and orientation. Given a set of training images, $\Gamma_1, \Gamma_2, \ldots, \Gamma_M$, where Γ_i is a $n \times n$ array of intensity values, their variation from the average, $\Psi = \frac{1}{M}\sum_{i=1}^{M}\Gamma_i$, is given by $\Phi_i = \Gamma_i - \Psi$. This set of vectors is then subjected to the Karhunen-Loève expansion, the result being a set of M eigenvectors u_k and eigenvalues λ_k of the covariance matrix $C = \frac{1}{M}\sum_{i=1}^{M}\Phi_i\Phi_i^T$. In representing a new image region, Γ, only $M_1 < M$ eigenvectors with the largest eigenvalues are used, thus the point in the eigenimage space corresponding to the new image is $\Omega = (\omega_1, \omega_2, \ldots, \omega_{M_1})$, where $\omega_k = u_k^T(\Gamma - \Psi)$, $k = 1, \ldots, M_1 < M$.
In a texture description, an image is viewed as a homogeneous 2D discrete random field, which by means of a Wold decomposition, is expressed as the sum of three orthogonal components. These components correspond to periodicity, directionality and randomness.
In creating a shape description, first a silhouette is extracted and a number of feature points on this are chosen (such as corners and high-curvature points). This feature points are then used as nodes in building a finite element model of the shape. Solving the following eigenvalue problem $K\phi_i = \omega_i^2 M\phi_i$, where M and K are the mass and stiffness matrices, respectively, the modes of the model are computed. These are the eigenvectors, ϕ_i, which are next used for determining a feature point correspondence between this new shape and some average shape.

Querying. To perform a query, the user selects some images from the grid of still images displayed and/or enters an annotation filter. From the images displayed, the user can select another query images and reiterate the search.

Matching. The distance between two eigenimage representations, Ω_1 and Ω_2, is $\epsilon_{ij}^2 = \|\Omega_i - \Omega_j\|^2$. Two shapes are compared by calculating the amount of strain energy needed to deform one shape to match the other.

Indexing. Prior to any database search, a few prototypes that span the image category are selected. For any image in the database, its distance to the average of the prototypes is computed and stored for future database search. At query time, the distance of the query image to the average is computed and the database is reordered according to this.

Result presentation. Images in the database are sorted by similarity with the query images and presented to the user page by page.

Applications. The face recognition technology of Photobook has been used by Viisage Technology in a FaceID package, which is used in several US police departments.

3.25 Picasso

Developer. Visual Information Processing Lab, University of Florence, Italy.

URL. `http://viplab.dsi.unifi.it/PICASSO`.

References. [50], [130].

Features. The Picasso system supports queries based on shape, color regions and their spatial relationships. The system exploits a pyramidal color segmentation of the database images, each level of the pyramid corresponding to a resolution level of the segmentation. At the lowest level, each pixel in the image is identified with one region, while at the highest level of the pyramid the entire image is represented by a single region. Image regions at level n are determined by iteratively merging adjacent regions from level $n-1$, minimizing the sum of all region energies. The energy E_R of a region R is given by $E_R = \alpha 1/A(R) + \beta D(R) + \gamma \sum_{R_i \in N(R)} 1/D(R \cup R_i)$, where $A(R)$ is the region's area, $D(R)$ is a measure of the uniformity in color of the pixels belonging to the region R, $N(R)$ denotes the set of regions adjacent to R and α, β and γ are positive real weights. This way, at the end of the segmentation process, each image is associated with N segmented images I_n, $n = 1 \ldots N$, which are represented using a multi-layered graph G. The nodes of G are the color regions of the N segmented images. There are two types of connections between these nodes: *intralevel* links between the nodes corresponding to adjacent regions in a segmented image I_n and *interlevel* links between a node corresponding to a region R_n^k of I_n and the nodes corresponding to regions of I_{n-1} that merged to form R_n^k. The description of a color region (graph node) include: a binary 187-dimensional color vector, the position of the region centroid, the region area (the fraction of region pixels in the total number of image pixels) and the region shape (the region is approximated by its best fit ellipse and the features used are the elongation and the major axis orientation). One property of the color vectors that helps in indexing and matching is that the color vector of a region R is computed as the union of the color vectors of the regions that merged to form R.

In order to allow queries by shape, the objects of interest in each image are bounded with their minimum enclosing rectangle (MER) during the database population step. Edge images (128×128 in size) of these rectangular areas are extracted through a Canny edge detection. Also, spatial relationships between objects' MER are represented using 2D strings [32]. The query contours drawn by the user are modeled by B-spline functions.

Querying. The system interface allows the user to select the type of search: by color regions or by shape. In the first case, regions can be indicated in two ways: either by drawing contours, which are then filled with colors chosen from a palette, or by loading a database image and tracing the contour of some relevant regions in this image. The user can also adjust the relevance of the region attributes (position, area, elongation and orientation). A query by shape is based on user drawn sketches, while for a query by texture patterns, the user has to pick an image from the database.

Matching. In a query by color regions, after a fast selection of the database images that contain all the colors of the query (see *Indexing*), the pyramidal structure of each candidate image is analyzed from top to bottom to find the best matching region for each query region. The matching score between a query region and a candidate image region is given by a weighted sum of distances between the computed region attributes (color, region centroid's position, area and shape). The similarity score between the query image and a candidate image is obtained by summing all the scores of the matched query regions.

In a shape based query, first images are filtered according to the spatial relationships and positions of the delimited MERs, based on the 2D string representation. 1D elastic matching is applied to the images that have passed this filtering step. If the sketch contains k contours, the systems warps each contour over the candidate image's shape located in the same relative position as the query contour. The similarity score between the deformed contour and the image object takes into account both the match M between the deformed contour and the edge image and the amount of elastic energy E used to warp the query contour. A gradient descent technique is used in minimizing $E - M$.

Indexing. In the color region queries, an expensive matching of the query against all database images is avoided by exploiting the color vectors. Because the color vector of the node in the highest level of the pyramidal color region representation includes colors of all the regions in the pyramid, a color index file is constructed. This contains the color vectors of the highest node of the pyramidal structure of each image and is used in the filtering step of the matching process, when only the images that contain all the colors of the query are selected for further inspection.

Result presentation. The query results are presented to the user in decreasing similarity order.

Relevance feedback. A query by sketch can be refined, for example by choosing one of the retrieved images and iterating a query by grey level intensity surface.

Applications. The system is used for the electronic cataloging of paintings and sculptures of museums and galleries in the area of central Italy.

3.26 PicHunter

Developer. NEC Research Institute, Princeton, NJ, USA.

References. [45].

Features. The current version of the systems uses color histogram and color spatial distribution along with hidden textual annotations. Besides a 64-bin HSV histogram, two other vectors – a 256-length HSV color autocorrellogram (CORR) and a 128-length RGB color-coherence vector (CCV) – are describing the color content of an image. The first 64 components of CORR represent the number of pixels of a particular color from the 64-quantized HSV color space having neighbors of the same color at distance 1. The rest of the vector is defined in the same way for distances 3, 5 and 7. CCV is made of 64 coherence pairs, each pair giving the number of coherent, and incoherent pixels of a particular discretized color in the RGB space. In order to classify pixels in one of the two categories, the image is first blurred slightly by replacing each pixel value with the average value of the pixels in its 3×3 neighborhood. Then, pixels are grouped in connected components. A pixel will be classified as coherent if the connected component it belongs to is larger than a fixed threshold. Keywords, selected from a set of 138 words, are associated with each image in the database population step and are represented as a boolean vector.

Querying. Retrieval is done with query by example.

Matching. The distance between individual features (color vectors or annotation lists represented as binary vectors) is the L_1 distance. These distances are scaled and combined in a global distance. The scaling factors are computed by maximizing the probability of a training set.

Relevance feedback. PicHunter implements a probabilistic relevance feedback mechanism, which tries to predict the target image the user wants based on his actions (the images he selects as similar to the target in each iteration of a query session). A vector is used for retaining each image's probability of being the target. This vector is updated at each iteration of the relevance feedback, based on the history of the session (images displayed by the system and user's actions in previous iterations). The updating formula is based on Bayes' rule. If the n database images are noted T_j, $j = 1, \ldots, n$, and the history of the session through iteration t is denoted $H_t = \{D_1, A_1, D_2, A_2, \ldots, D_t, A_t\}$, with D_j and A_j being the images displayed by the system and, respectively, the action taken by the user at the iteration j, then the iterative update of the probability estimate of an image T_i being the target, given the history H_t, is:

$$\begin{aligned} P(T = T_i|H_t) &= P(T = T_i|D_t, A_t, H_{t-1}) \\ &= \frac{P(A_t|T = T_i, D_t, H_{t-1})P(T = T_i|H_{t-1})}{\sum_{j=1}^{n} P(A_t|T = T_j, D_t, H_{t-1})P(T = T_j|H_{t-1})} \end{aligned}$$

In computing the probability of a user to take a certain action A_t given the history so far and the fact that the target is indeed T_i, namely $P(A_t|T = T_i, D_t, H_{t-1})$, a few models were tested. One approach is to estimate the probability of the user to pick an image X_a from $X_1, \ldots, X_{n_t}$ by

$$p_{softmin}(A = a|X_1, \ldots, X_{n_t}, T) = \frac{exp(-d(X_a, T)/\sigma)}{\sum_{i=1}^{n_t} exp(-d(X_i, T)/\sigma)},$$

and, in the case of choosing any number of images, to assume that each image is selected independently according to a $p_{softmin}$.

Result presentation. While older versions were displaying the n_t images with the highest probability of being the target, in the newer version the images selected for display are determined by minimizing the expected number of future iterations estimated by entropy.

Applications. The system was tested with a database gathering images from 45 CD's of Corel stock photographs.

3.27 PicSOM

Developer. Laboratory of Computer and Information Sciences, Helsinki University of Technology, Finland.

URL. `http://www.cis.hut.fi/picsom`. A demo of the system is available there too.

References. [98].

Features. The following features are computed for a center region, and four regions along the sides. The average R, G, B values give a 15-dimensional vector. The color moments (mean, variance, skewness) of each color channel give a 45-dimensional vector. The Y-values of the YIQ color representation of every pixel's 8-neighborhood are examined, and the estimated probabilities for each neighbor being brighter than the center pixel give a 40 dimensional texture feature vector. After applying the Sobel edge detector, each edge pixel direction is put in a 8-bins histogram, which gives a 40-dimensional vector.

Also, the image was normalized 512 × 512 pixels, and the binarized edge image was transformed with the Fourier transform. The magnitude image of the Fourier spectrum was low-pass filtered and decimated by a factor 32, resulting in a 128-dimensional vector.

Querying. Querying is an iterative process with relevance feedback. The query begins with a fixed selection of representative images. Query improvement is achieved by relevance feedback.

Matching. The matching is based on the Self-Organizing Map (SOM). The SOM consist of a regular grid of units, each having a feature vector. The SOM is fed with all database images by a sequential regression process, which makes that images are ordered on the grid so that similar images are close to each other. To speed up processing, a multi-level SOM is used to represent the image database. A unit in a higher level SOM represents a cluster of similar images. The distance between the units in the SOM is the Euclidean distance between there feature vectors.

Indexing. The indexing data structure is in fact the array of the SOM.

Relevance feedback. Each SOM level is treated as a two-dimensional matrix formed of values describing the user's responses to the contents of the seen map units. The matrices are low-pass filtered to spread the responses to the neighboring map units.

Result presentation. Starting from the SOM unit having the largest positive convolved response, PicSOM retrieves the representative images associated with the map units. If that image has not already been shown to the user, it is presented in the next round.

3.28 PicToSeek

Developer. Department of Computer Science, University of Amsterdam, The Netherlands.

URL. `http://www.science.uva.nl/research/isis/pictoseek/`.

A demo of the system is available at `http://zomax.wins.uva.nl:5345/ret_user/`.

References. [61].

Features. Color and shape invariants are defined to be used as features in content based queries independent of camera viewpoint, geometry of the objects and illumination conditions. Under the assumption of a dichromatic reflection model, the effect of various imaging conditions on the different color features is analyzed. (In this model, reflection is used to determine how color clusters are formed in the RGB color space by pixels coming from the same uniformly colored surface of the object.)

Assuming a white illumination and a matte object surface, a basic set of irreducible color invariants is formed by $\{R/G, B/R, G/B\}$. Also, it is proven that the normalized color model rgb and a newly defined model $c_4c_5c_6$, with $c_4 = (R-G)/(R+B)$, $c_5 = (R-B)/(R+B)$ and $c_6 = (G-B)/(G+B)$, are independent of the viewpoint, illumination direction, illumination intensity and surface orientation of matte objects. The set of color invariants, independent of viewpoint, used in the case of a shiny surfaced object, are $l_4 = |R-G|/(|R-G|+|B-R|+|G-B|)$, $l_5 = |R-B|/(|R-G|+|B-R|+|G-B|)$, $l_6 = |G-B|/(|R-G|+|B-R|+|G-B|)$. Based on the above color invariants, normalized color histograms are computed, H_A defined on the c_4, c_5 and c_6 axes and H_B on l_4, l_5, and l_6 axes. Color invariant gradients are defined using a multi-band approach and a histogram H_C of $l_4l_5l_6$ color edges is computed. That is because the color gradient for $l_4l_5l_6$ is the one that measures the presence of material edges (not shadow or highlight edges) in an image.

The shape invariants used are the angle between two color edges (invariant under rigid motion plus scaling) and the cross-ratio (projective invariant) between four color edges originating in the same point. A 1D histogram H_D is constructed on the discretized angle values, and a similar one H_E on the cross ratio values. Color and shape invariants are also combined in a 4D histogram H_F such that $H_F(i,j,k,l)$ counts the number of color edge maxima points of (i,j,k) color and generating an angle l.

Querying. The query image can be selected from the database collected by the system's Web crawlers or brought in by the user by giving a URL address. Before submitting the query, the user has to select the desired invariance, which indicates to the system how to choose the invariants in computing the similarity. Queries by user-specified feature values are also allowed.

Matching. The similarity measure between a query histogram H_j^Q and a database image histogram H_j^I is the normalized intersection

$d(H_j^Q, H_j^I) = (\sum_{k=1}^{n} min\{H_j^Q(k), H_j^I(k)\})/(\sum_{k=1}^{n} H_j^Q(k))$,
with $j \in \{A,B,C,D,E,F\}$ and n is the number of nonzero bins in H_j^Q.

Result presentation. The retrieved images are shown without explicit order.

3.29 QBIC (Query By Image Content)

Developer. IBM Almaden Research Center, San Jose, CA.

URL. `http://wwwqbic.almaden.ibm.com/`.

References. [125].

Features. Color features computed are: the 3D average color vector of an object or the whole image in RGB, YIQ, Lab, and Munsell color space and a 256-dimensional RGB color histogram. If x is an n-dimensional color histogram and $C = [c_1 c_2 \dots c_n]$ is a $3 \times n$ matrix whose columns represent the RGB values of the n quantized colors, the average color vector x_{avg} is $C\ x$. The texture features used in QBIC are modified versions of the coarseness, contrast, and directionality features proposed by Tamura [169].

The shape features consist of shape area, circularity, eccentricity, major axis orientation and a set of algebraic moment invariants. The major axis orientation and the eccentricity are computed from the second order covariance matrix of the boundary pixels: the major axis orientation as the direction of the largest eigenvector and eccentricity as the ratio of the smallest eigenvalue to the largest one. For the database images, these shape features are extracted for all the object contours, semiautomatically computed in the database population step. In this process, the user enters an approximate object outline, which is automatically aligned with the nearby image edges, using the active contours technique. In this object identification step, the user can also associate text to the outlined objects.

The 18 algebraic moment invariants are the eigenvalues of the matrices $M_{[2,2]}$, $M_{[2,3]} \times M_{[3,2]}$, $M_{[3,3]}$, $M_{[3,4]} \times M_{[4,3]}$, $M_{[4,4]}$, $M_{[4,5]} \times M_{[5,4]}$, where the elements of $M_{[i,j]}$ are scaled factors of the central moments.

QBIC also implemented a method of retrieving images based on a rough user sketch. For this purpose, images in the database are represented by a reduced binary map of edge points. This is obtained as follows: first, the color image is converted to a single band luminance; using a Canny edge detector, the binary edge image is computed and is next reduced to size 64×64. Finally this reduced image is thinned.

Querying. QBIC allows queries based on example images, user-constructed sketches or/and selected color and texture patterns. In the last case, the user chooses colors or textures from a sampler. The percentage of a desired color in an image is adjusted by moving sliders.

Matching. For the average color, the distance between a query object and database object is a weighted Euclidean distance, where the weights are the inverse standard deviation for each component over the samples in the database. In matching two color histograms, two distance measures are used: one low-dimensional, easy to compute (the average color distance) and one much more computationally expensive (the quadratic histogram distance). The first one (which is computed for all the images in the database) acts as a filter, limiting the expensive matching computation to the small set of images retrieved by the first matching. The average color distance is $d^2_{avg}(x, y) = (x_{avg} - y_{avg})^t(x_{avg} - y_{avg})$. The histogram quadratic distance is given by $d^2_{hist}(x, y) = (x-y)^t A(x-y)$, where the symmetric color similarity matrix A is given by $a_{ij} = 1 - d_{ij}/d_{max}$, with d_{ij} being the L_2 distance between the colors i and j in the RGB space and $d_{max} = max_{i,j} d_{ij}$. The texture distance is a weighted Euclidean distance, with the weighting factors being the inverse variances for each of the three texture components over the entire database. Two shapes are matched also by a similar weighted Euclidean distance between shape feature vectors.

In a query by sketch, after reducing the binary sketch image drawn by the user to size 64×64, a correlation based matching is performed, a kind of template matching. This is done by partitioning the user sketch into 8×8 blocks of 8×8 pixels and find the maximum correlation of each block of the sketch within a search area of 16×16 pixels in the image database (this is done by shifting the 8×8 block in the search area). This local correlation score is computed on the pixel level using logical operations.

The matching score of a database image is the sum of the correlation scores of all local blocks.

Indexing. QBIC was one of the first systems that applied multidimensional indexing to enhance the speed performance of the system. The average color and the texture features (both 3D vectors) are indexed using R^*-trees. The 18-dimensional moment-based shape feature vector is first reduced using the KL transform and then indexed by using R^*-trees.

Result presentation. The best matches are presented in decreasing similarity order with (optionally) the matching score aside.

Relevance feedback. Any retrieved image can be used as a seed for a subsequent query by example.

3.30 Quicklook2

Developer. CNR Institute of Multimedia Information Technologies, Milan, Italy.

URL. `http://www.itim.mi.cnr.it/Linee/Linea1/Sottolinea3/`.

References. [37].

Features. Besides text descriptors, Quicklook2 uses the following content-based features. The color histogram of 64 bins. The color coherence vector in Lab color space, quantized into 64 colors, where pixels are coherent if they belong to a large similarly colored region; the image is first blurred by averaging a 3×3 neighborhood. The percentage of skin-colored pixels. The 'spatial chromaticity histogram': bin i gives the ratio $h(i)$ of pixels having color i, the relative coordinates of the baricenter $\mathbf{b(i)}$ of these pixels, and the standard deviation $\sigma(i)$ of these pixels' distance to the baricenter. The co-occurrence of colors in Lab color space, quantized into 11 colors: red, orange, yellow, green, blue, purple, pink, brown, black, gray, white. The moments of inertia (mean, variance, skewness, kurtosis) of the color distribution in Lab space. Contrast information at Canny edge pixels: the percentage of low, medium, and high contrast pixels, the thresholds on the gradient strengths corresponding to medium and high contrast, the number of connected regions with high contrast contours, and the percentage of medium contrast edge pixels connected to high contrast edges. Texture features based on the 'neighborhood gray tone difference matrix' [10]: coarseness, contrast, busyness, complexity, and strength. The mean and variance of the absolute values of the Daubechies wavelet transform coefficients of the luminance of the subimages at the first three levels of resolution. The histogram of 72 bins of directions of high gradient pixels on Canny edges. The Hu moment invariants [84]. After quantization into 11 colors: the number of color regions, the distribution of these regions around the center, x, and y axis.

Querying. The user initially selects a query image. The features of this image are taken for the first search. The user can than indicate which images are relevant. From these relevant image a new query feature vector is composed, see below.

Matching. The distance between two spatial chromaticity histograms h_1, h_2 of length k is defined as

$$\sum_{i=1}^{k} \min\{h_1(i), h_2(i)\}(1 - d(\mathbf{b_1(i)}, \mathbf{b_1(i)})\sqrt{\mathbf{2}}/\mathbf{2})+$$
$$\min\{\sigma_1(i), \sigma_2(i)\}/\max\{\sigma_1(i), \sigma_2(i)\}.$$

The distance measure for any of the other features is the L_1 distance. Each distances measure d_j is normalized by a factor $\mu_j + K\sigma_j$, with μ_j and σ_j the average and the standard deviation over all images, and K, which affects the number of outliers, set to 3. The total distance between two images is a weighted sum of the feature distance measures d_j.

Indexing. In a preprocessing step, the distance of all database objects to m reference objects are computed. At query time, the distances d_i, $i = 1, \ldots, m$ of the query to these reference objects is also computed. With an SQL query, those database objects are retrieved that lie within some range from each d_i. After this filtering, these database objects are compared to the query directly.

Result presentation. The results are listed in decreasing order of similarity.

Relevance feedback. The innovative part of the system is the relevance feedback method. After the relevant images are selected, each of their features contributes to the new query feature vector if its distance to the average over the relevant images' feature is sufficiently large (three times the standard deviation). The new query feature vector is the average of the contributing features.

3.31 Shoebox

Developer. AT&T Laboratories, Cambridge, UK. The development was started at Olivetti and Oracle Research Laboratory.

URL. `http://www.uk.research.att.com/dart/shoebox/`.

References. [115].

Features. The images are annotated by keywords using speech recognition. The automatic features extracted are the average color in HSV color space, and the variances in each of the color channels of regions. The regions are either resulting from color segmentation, or a fixed partitioning of the image, or the overlay of both.

Querying. Querying can be done with the spoken annotations. Another way is to select a region from an image in the database to find similar images.

Matching. The Euclidean distance between feature vectors for use with the M-tree. For use with a B-tree, the feature space is quantized, and the corresponding values are used in an inverted index.

Indexing. Both the B-tree and the M-tree are used for indexing.

Result presentation. When querying with regions, the system can highlight those regions in the resulting images that match the query region.

Applications. The system is meant as a tool to manage personal photo collections.

Performance. The M-tree indexing outperforms the B-tree indexing.

3.32 SIMBA (Search Images By Appearance)

Developer. Institute for Pattern Recognition and Image Processing, Freiburg University, Germany.

URL. `http://simba.informatik.uni-freiburg.de/`. A demo is available at the same address.

References. [150].

Features. The system uses a histogram of a function f of transformed local pixel patterns of image $I(x, y)$, taken over all rigid motions g. For example, $f(I)$ could be $I(0,1) \cdot I(2,0)$, and the histograms could be constructed of the values $g_{t_0,t_1,\phi}(I(0,1)) \cdot g_{t_0,t_1,\phi}(I(2,0))$, $t_0 = 0,\ldots,n$, $t_1 = 0,\ldots,m$, $\phi = 0, P-12\pi/P$. This is based on the observation that the integration over all transformations g (Haar integral) of $f(g(I))$ makes f invariant under these transformations. The histogram is used rather than the integral, to keep more local information. By combining different functions f and different color layers (RGB in the online demo, however, also HSV, luminance and chromaticities are supported) a multidimensional histogram is built. A fuzzy version of the histogram was developed to get rid of the discontinuities of the histogram operator at bin boundaries. The evaluation of the features is speeded up by Monte Carlo estimation instead of a full calculation.

Querying. The user is presented with a selectable number (1-25) of random images from the database. By selecting one of these, a query for similar images is started. Alternatively, the user can specify a URL for his own query image, whose size must be comparable to the size of the database images (384x256).

Matching. The system provides histogram intersection (used in the demo), as well as χ^2, L_1, and L_2 distances for matching.

Indexing. No indexing data structure is used.

Result presentation. The results of a query are shown in decreasing order of match row by row. The user may specify resolution and number of rows/columns for the results, before starting a query. The result display can be used for a new query by clicking on one of the displayed images (to come iteratively closer to the desired image type) or by specifying a new URL.

3.33 SMURF (Similarity-based Multimedia Retrieval Framework)

Developer. Center for Geometry, Imaging, and Virtual Environments, Institute of Information and Computing Sciences, Utrecht University, The Netherlands.

URL. `http://give-lab.cs.uu.nl`.

References. [180].

Features. It is a framework that incorporates color, texture, and shape, but the system is primarily oriented towards shape-based retrieval research. In particular there are demo's for polyline matching, and weighted point set matching.

Querying. The search is started by selecting an image from a random selection. The user can select a new image from the search results so as to narrow down to the target images.

Matching. Matching of two polylines is done by computing the area between the two corresponding turning angle functions, and minimizing over rotations (vertical shift of the function), and starting position (horizontal shift). The weighted point set matching is done with a pseudometric, the Proportional Transportation Distance. Unlike the Earth Movers Distance, it obeys the triangle inequality for sets of unequal weight, which is essential for the indexing method used.

Indexing. The triangle inequality and similarity of similarity measures is used to make the search more efficient. This is based on the following observation. Consider a shape or point set A_1 that closely matches a query A_q: $d(A_1, A_q)$ is small. Let A_r be some reference shape, called vantage object. If the triangle inequality holds, $d(A_r, A_q) \leq d(A_r, A_1) + d(A_1, A_q)$, then we know that $d(A_r, A_q) - d(A_r, A_1)$ is small as well. We can measure the distance between a database shape A_1 and a query A_q by comparing their distances from a vantage object A_r. The computation of the latter distances can be done off-line for all A_i. So at run-time the computation of a single $d(A_r, A_q)$ yields all A_i that resemble A_r as much as A_q, including those that resemble A_q. Using multiple vantage objects, say m, increases precision, recall is always 100%. A similar approach was taken in FIDS [19]. In SMURF, the search is done with an optimal approximate k-nearest neighbor search in the m-dimensional 'vantage space' of distances. In this way, the number of expensive similarity measures between shapes is reduced to m. The search further only takes cheap distance computations in vantage space.

Result presentation. The results are shown in decreasing order of match score.

Applications. The polyline matching is applied to about 70,000 polylines from a collection of hieroglyphics that is used as a font for a hieroglyphic text processor. The weighted point set matching is used for searching in a collection of 1100 fish contours.

3.34 SQUID (Shape Queries Using Image Databases)

Developer. Centre for Vision, Speech, and Signal Processing, University of Surrey, UK.

URL. `http://www.ee.surrey.ac.uk/Research/VSSP/imagedb/demo.html`.

References. [119].

Features. The boundary contour extracted from an image is represented by three global shape parameters (eccentricity, circularity and aspect ratio of the Curvature Scale Space image) and a descriptor obtained from the CSS image. The CSS image of a closed planar curve, Γ, is computed by repeatedly convolving its natural parameterization, $\{(x(u), y(u)) \mid u \in [0,1]\}$, with a Gaussian function of increasing standard deviation σ and representing the curvature zero-crossing points (inflection points) of the resulting curve, $\Gamma_\sigma = \{(x(u) * g(u,\sigma), y(u) * g(u,\sigma)) \mid u \in [0,1]\}$, in the (u, σ) plane. The shape descriptor is made of the maxima of the CSS image contours.

Querying. The user selects one of the displayed object boundaries in order to generate a query for similar contours.

Matching. First, from the database are chosen those models whose global parameters are sufficiently close to the query global parameters. To these images a CSS matching algorithm is applied. This consists of first finding a circular shift of one of the two sets of maxima so that they best match the other set and then computing the matching score as the sum of the Euclidean distances between the matched pairs plus the vertical coordinates of the unmatched maxima.

Result presentation. The system displays the first n matched images in decreasing similarity order. Under each retrieved image, an integer match value is shown.

Applications. The system database consists of 1100 images of marine creatures on a uniform background.

3.35 Surfimage

Developer. INRIA, Rocquencourt, France.

URL. `http://www-rocq.inria.fr/imedia/index_UK.html`.

References. [124].

Features. Surfimage gives the possibility of combining various low-level and high-level features. The low-level features are RGB color histogram, edge-orientation histogram computed after applying a Canny edge detector, texture signature derived from the gray-level co-occurrence matrix, Fourier transform, and Wavelet transform. High-level features include eigenimages (see Photobook), deformable intensity surfaces, and intensity surface curvature histogram. The latter is a normalized histogram of

$$S_I(p) = \frac{1}{2} - \frac{1}{\pi} \arctan \frac{k_1(p) + k_2(p)}{k_1(p) - k_2(p)}$$

at each point $p = (x, y, I(x, y))$ over the entire image, where k_1, k_2 are the principal curvature values.

Querying. The user selects image features and appropriate similarity measures from the lists displayed and specifies weights to define the importance of each feature in the retrieval. He also can select a database (among the databases available are the MIT face database used in Photobook, the MIT Vistex database of textures, a paintings database, the BTphoto database of city/country scenes and a combined database).

Matching. Various similarity metrics are implemented in Surfimage. Among them are standard metrics, such as the L_p distances (most often used are L_1 and L_2), the cosine metric $d_{cos}(x, y) = 1 - x \cdot y/\|x\|\|y\|$, or statistical metrics such as the Hellinger metric

$$d_H(x, y) = 1 - \sum_{i=1}^{n} \sqrt{\frac{x_i\, y_i}{|x||y|}},$$

where $\|x\|$ is the L_2 norm and $|x|$ is the L_1 norm of the vector x. For histograms the intersection metric is used.

In the case of choosing more than one feature for the query, the corresponding similarity measures are combined in a final weighted measure. Before this, some of the distance measures are normalized so that they have values in $[0, 1]$. If μ_i and σ_i are the mean and standard deviation of the distance d for the feature i, this distance is normalized to: $d_n(x^i, y^i) = [d(x^i, y^i) - (\mu_i - 3\sigma_i)]/6\sigma_i$.

Relevance feedback. Surfimage has a relevance feedback mechanism, which takes into consideration both relevant and nonrelevant examples from the user, in a statistical approach that estimates the distribution of relevant images.

3.36 SYNAPSE (SYNtactic APpearance Search Engine)

Developer. Center for Intelligent Information Retrieval, University of Massachusetts, Amherst, MA.

URL. `http://hobart.cs.umass.edu/~mmedia/`.

A demo of the system is available at the address `http://cowarie.cs.umass.edu/~demo/Demo.html`.

References. [111].

Features. Queries are made on the visual appearance of the objects in the image, defined as the shape of the intensity surface and represented using the outputs of a set of Gaussian derivative filters. More precisely, each image is filtered at uniformly sampled points with Gaussian derivative up to the order 2. Thus, for each sampled point $p = (x, y)$ of intensity $I(p)$, the so-called 2-jet at this point is given by the vector $J^2[I](p, \sigma) = \{I_\sigma(p), I_{x,\sigma}(p), I_{y,\sigma}(p), I_{x^2,\sigma}(p), I_{xy,\sigma}(p), I_{y^2,\sigma}(p)\}$, where

$I_{x^i y^i,\sigma}(p)$ is the image convoluted with the (i, j)-th partial derivative of the Gaussian function of scale

σ: $I_{x^i y^i,\sigma}(p) = I(p) * \sigma^{i+j} \partial^{i+j} G(p, \sigma)/\partial x^i \partial y^i$, $i, j \in \{0, 1, 2\}$.

From this vector, four differential invariants are computed: $d_1^\sigma = I_x^2 + I_y^2$, $d_2^\sigma = I_{x^2} + I_{y^2}$, $d_3^\sigma = I_{x^2} I_x^2 + 2I_{xy} I_x I_y + I_{y^2} I_y^2$, $d_4^\sigma = I_{x^2}^2 + 2I_{xy}^2 + I_{y^2}^2$. Computing these four invariants at three different scales, $\sigma_1, \sigma_2, \sigma_3$, a multi-scale invariant vector D is generated for each sampled point p. Along with each multi-scale invariant vector D, the coordinates (x, y) of the corresponding sampled point and the number i of the image are also stored.

Querying. Querying is done by example.

Matching. Matching is done in two phases. First, for every invariant vector D_n of the query image, a number of invariant vectors stored in the database are found so that they lie in the range $[D_n - t, D_n + t]$. This is done by finding for each component $D_n(j)$ a list of invariant vectors, whose j-component lies in the interval $[D_n(j) - t(j), D_n(j) + t(j)]$ and intersecting the lists.

In the second phase, a spatial check is performed on the list of candidate images. For each sampled point q_m of the query image, the number S_m of query points whose Euclidean distance to the q_m is within a threshold factor of the Euclidean distance of their corresponding points in the candidate image. The score of the candidate image is given by $\max_m S_m$.

Indexing. An index is created on each of the 12 coordinates of the invariant vector D. Instead of storing each invariant vector in one record of the form (i, x, y, D), 12 smaller tables (inverted file lists), each with 4 columns $(D(p), i, x, y)$, are generated. Each inverted file list is stored in a binary tree sorted on the first column.

Result presentation. Images are showed in decreasing similarity score.

Relevance feedback. The search can be refined by marking the relevant images found among the results of a query and reiterate the query.

3.37 TODAI (Typographic Ornament Database And Identification)

Developer. Electrical Engineering Department, EPFL, Switzerland, and later the Intelligent Systems Laboratory, Halmstad University, Sweden.

URL. `http://www.unil.ch/BCU/docs/collecti/res_prec/en/wtres/todai_doc.html`.

References. [114].

Features. The image is first decomposed into six orientation images. Each orientation image is result of applying a filter that passes edges with a specified orientation. Thus, an orientation image contains information about the presence in the original image of linear structure in the direction of the pass orientation. The projection of the orientation image in the direction of the pass orientation is called an orientation radiogram. Six fixed directions are chosen to make radiograms. Each radiogram is represented by a feature vector of the real parts and the absolute values of the imaginary parts of the first ten Fourier coefficients. The absolute value operation provides invariance to flipping of the image.

Querying. The user can specify the location of a query image. Additional criteria such as the size, use and nature of the ornament can be indicated. There is a possibility to make an advanced search combining keywords and the image content.

Matching. The similarity between two images is the sum of the Euclidean distances of the six feature vectors.

Result presentation. The best match is shown, the user can browse through the list of next matches.

Applications. The system is used in Passe-Partout, the International Bank of Printers' Ornaments , which stores 2316 images.

3.38 VIR Image Engine

The VIR Image Engine is an extensible framework for building content based image retrieval systems.

Developer. Virage Inc.

URL. `http://www.virage.com/products/vir-irw.html`.

References. [13].

Features. A basic concept is that of a *primitive*, which denotes a feature's type, computation and matching distance. Five abstract data types are defined: global values and histograms, local values and histograms, and graphs. The VIR Image Engine provides a set of general primitives, such as global color, local color, texture and shapes. Apart from these, various domain specific primitives can be created when developing an application. When defining such a primitive, the developer supplies a function for computing the primitive's feature data from the raw image.

Querying and Result presentation. The VIR Image Engine provides a set of GUI tools necessary for the development of a user interface. These include facilities for image insertion, image query, weight adjustment for re-query, inclusion of keywords, and support for several popular image file formats. Another available component, the query canvas, allows queries-by-sketch; it consists of a bitmap editor where the user can sketch a picture with drawing tools and color it using the colors from a palette. Also, the user can bring onto the canvas an image from an existing collection and modify it using the same drawing tools. Queries can be performed on various user-defined combinations of primitives.

Matching. When defining a new primitive, a function for computing the similarity between two sets of feature data previously extracted must also be supplied by the developer. When comparing two images, for each primitive in the current query combination, a similarity score is computed using the distance function defined within the primitive. These individual scores are combined in an overall score using a set of weights in a way characteristic to the application. This score is then stored in a *score structure*, which contains also the individual similarity scores for each primitive. This allows a quick recomputation of the overall score for a new set of weights.

Relevance feedback. A sort of relevance feedback is obtained by searching for matches to a fixed query image for different sets of weights.

Indexing. The storage of feature data for all primitives is the responsibility of the application developer.

Applications. The system was integrated into databases from Sybase, Object Design, and Objectivity, and added as a component to the Oracle DBMS. The AltaVista Photofinder and Illustra's Visual Intelligence system are two applications of Virage technology.

3.39 VisualSEEk

Developer. Image and Advanced Television Lab, Columbia University, NY.

URL. `http://www.ctr.columbia.edu/VisualSEEk/`.

References. [158].

Features. In the database population step, each image is automatically decomposed into regions of equally dominant colors. For each region, feature properties and spatial properties are retained for the subsequent queries. A query consists of finding the images that contain the most similar arrangements of similar regions.
The color region extraction uses the back-projection technique. The first step is the selection of a color set. This is a 166-dimensional binary vector c, which defines a selection of 166 colors in the HSV color space. From a given image I, another image B is generated by $B[x, y] = \max_j a[k, j]c[j]$, where $k \in \{0, \ldots, 165\}$ is the index of the color of the pixel (x, y) in the image I and $a[k, j]$ is the similarity between two colors (with the indices k and j) in the HSV space. Next the image B is filtered and spatially localized color regions are extracted. Along with the color set used for back-projection, the region centroid,

area (defined as the number of pixels in the region) and the width and height of the minimum bounding rectangle are also stored.

Querying. To start a query, the user sketches a number of regions, positions and dimensions them on the grid and selects a color for each region. Also, the user can indicate boundaries for location and size and/or spatial relationships between regions. After the system returns the thumbnail images of the best matches, the user is allowed to search by example using the returned images.

Matching. To find the matches of a query image with a single region, queries on color set, region absolute location, area and spatial extent are first done independently. The color set similarity is computed by $d(c_q, c_t) = (c_q - c_t)^t A(c_q - c_t)$, where c_q, c_t are two color sets and $A = (a[i, j])$ is the color similarity matrix. If the user has defined spatial boundaries for the query region, then its distance to a target region is 0 if the target region centroid falls inside this boundaries, and is given by the Euclidean distance between the centroids otherwise. The distance in area between two regions is the absolute value of the difference, while the distance between the minimum bounding rectangles, (w_q, h_q) and (w_t, h_t), of two regions is the L_2 metric. The results of these queries are intersected and from the obtained candidate set, the best matching images are taken by minimizing a total distance given by the weighted sum of the four distances mentioned.
If the query image consists of a number of regions, in absolute or relative location, then for each region positioned in absolute location, a query like that described above is made, and for regions positioned by relative location individual queries on all attributes except location are performed. For the intersection of all this query results, the relative spatial relations specified by the user are evaluated using 2D string representation [32].

Indexing. The color set distance can be written as $d(c_q, c_t) = \mu_q + \mu_t - 2c_q^t r_t$, where $\mu_q = c_q^t A c_q$, $\mu_t = c_t^t A c_t$ and $r_t = A c_t$. For each target region, μ_t and $r_t[m]$, $m \in \{0, \ldots, 165\}$, are indexed individually. The centroids of the image regions are indexed using a quadtree. For the indexing of the minimum bounding rectangles, R-tree are used.

Result presentation. The results of a query are displayed in decreasing similarity order. Under each retrieved image, the distance to the query image is indicated.

Performance. Another system, SaFe [152], was developed in order to improve the performances of VisualSEEk. SaFe was suppose to extend the query capabilities to other features, such as texture, and to incorporate more powerful spatial indexing techniques. There is no indication that this has been done. The two systems seems to differ only in the user interface.

3.40 WebSEEk

Developer. Image and Advanced Television Lab, Columbia University, NY.

URL. `http://www.ctr.columbia.edu/WebSEEk/`.

References. [152].

Features. WebSEEk makes text-based and color based queries through a catalogue of images and videos collected from the Web. Color is represented by means of a normalized 166-bin histogram in the HSV color space, see VisualSEEk.

Querying. The user initiates a query by choosing a subject from the available catalogue or entering a topic. The results of the query may be used for a color query in the whole catalogue or for sorting the result list by decreasing color similarity to the selected item. Also, the user has the possibility of manually modifying an image/video color histogram before reiterating the search.

Matching. The distance between a query color histogram h_q and a target histogram h_t is given by $d(h_q, h_t) = (h_q - h_t)^t A(h_q - h_t) \approx \mu_q + \mu_t - 2\sum_{k\, with\, h_q[k] \geq \tau} h_q[k] r_t[k]$, where $A = (a[i, j])$ is a color similarity matrix, $\mu_q = h_q^t A h_q$, $\mu_t = h_t^t A h_t$, $r_t = Ah_t$ and τ defines a threshold for choosing the most significant colors in the approximated distance.

Indexing. For all the database images, μ_t and $r_t[k]$, $k \in \{0, \ldots, 165\}$ are computed and indexed individually.

Result presentation. Images retrieved are displayed page by page in a descending similarity order. A manipulation (union, intersection, subtraction) of the search result lists, in order to reiterate a query, is possible.

Relevance feedback. The user has the possibility of selecting positive and negative examples from the result of a query in order to reformulate the query. If the set of relevant images is denoted by I_r and the set of nonrelevant images is I_n then the new query histogram at the $(k+1)$th feedback iteration is computed by $h_q^{k+1} = \|\alpha h_q^k + \beta \sum_{i \in I_r} h_i - \gamma \sum_{j \in I_n} h_j\|$.

3.41 WebSeer

Developer. Department of Computer Science, University of Chicago, Illinois, USA.

References. [164].

Features. The images collected from the Web are submitted to a number of color tests in order to separate photographs from drawings. Some simple tests measure the number of different colors in the image, the fraction of pixels which have one of the N most frequent colors for a given threshold N, the fraction of pixels with transition value (the largest L_1 distance between a pixel and one of its neighbors in the RGB space) greater than a threshold T, the fraction of pixels with saturation level (the difference between the maximum and the minimum value of the RGB color bands) greater than a threshold T, and the ratio of the image dimensions. A more elaborate test creates first an average color histogram for graphics, H_g, and one for photographs, H_p, using two large sets of images. Defining the correlation between two normalized RGB histograms, A and B, as $C(A,B) = \sum_{i=0}^{15}\sum_{j=0}^{15}\sum_{k=0}^{15} A_{i,j,k}B_{i,j,k}$, an image with a color histogram H_i gains a score to the test equal to $s = C(H_i, H_p)/(C(H_i, H_p)+C(H_i, H_g))$. Two similar tests are also made using the farthest neighbour histograms and the saturation histograms instead of the color histograms.

Images determined to be photographs are subjected to a face detector based on a neural network. Keywords are extracted from the image file name, captions, hyperlinks, alternate text and HTML titles.

Querying. The user gives keywords describing the contents of the desired images, and optionally specifies some image characteristics such as dimensions, file size or whether he is looking for photographs or drawings. In the case the user is looking for people, he must indicate the number of faces as well as the size of the portrait.

Matching. To classify an image as photograph or graphics, the color tests are combined using multiple decision trees constructed using a training set of hand-classified images. They are binary trees whose internal nodes contain the next test the image should be submitted to and a threshold to direct the search by comparing the test result with the threshold. In each leaf we find a probability estimate that the image is a photograph. Computing the mean of the results got from all decision trees and comparing this with a threshold, a decision is taken whether the image falls in one category or the other.

Result presentation. The thumbnails of the resulting images are displayed by decreasing size of the face in the case of searching for portraits. Otherwise, there is no explicit order of the retrieved images. The user has access to the Web page where the image was collected from, through a page icon aside the displayed thumbnail.

3.42 WISE (Wavelet Image Search Engine)

Developer. Department of Computer Science, Stanford Univerity.

URL. `http://www-db.stanford.edu/~wangz/project/imsearch/`.

A demo of the system is available at `http://bergman.stanford.edu/~zwang/project/imsearch/WBIIS.html`.

References. [183].

Features. The system, also called WBIIS (Wavelet-Based Image Indexing and Searching), performs queries on color layout information encoded using Daubechies wavelet transforms. In a preprocessing step, the image is rescaled to 128×128 pixels and converted from RGB color space representation to another color space. This color space, defined by $C_1 = (R+G+B)/3$, $C_2 = (R+(max-B))/2$, $C_3 = (R+2*(max-G)+B)/4$, with max the maximum possible value for each RGB color component, is selected because of its similarity to the opponent color axes used by the human visual system. On each of the three color components, a 4-layer 2D fast wavelet transform using Daubechies wavelets is applied. From the resulting 128×128 matrices, denoted as W_{C_1}, W_{C_2}, and W_{C_3}, each 16×16 upper left corner is stored as part of the feature vector (the 8×8 upper left corner, representing the lowest frequency bands in the wavelet transforms, accounts for object configurations in the image, while the three surrounding 8×8 submatrices represent detail information). Also, the standard deviation, σ_{C_i}, of the 8×8 upper left corner of W_{C_i} is computed and stored as part of the feature vector.

Querying. Querying is done by example, where the query image is either a database image or a hand drawn sketch. Also low resolution images or partial images (images that contain non-specified areas represented by black rectangles) can be query images to the system.

Matching. The matching process is performed in two steps. In the first step, the standard deviations computed for the query image, $\sigma^q_{C_i}$, are compared with the corresponding values, $\sigma^i_{C_i}$, stored for each database image. If the acceptance criterion, $(\sigma^q_{C_1}\beta < \sigma^i_{C_1} < \sigma^q_{C_1}/\beta) \vee ((\sigma^q_{C_2}\beta < \sigma^i_{C_2} < \sigma^q_{C_2}/\beta) \wedge (\sigma^q_{C_3}\beta < \sigma^i_{C_3} < \sigma^q_{C_3}/\beta))$, with the threshold β usually set to 0.5, is not achieved, the distance between the two images is set to 1. In the second step, the images that passed the first matching phase are compared to the query using a weighted Euclidean distance between wavelet transform coefficients: $\sum_{m=1}^{2}\sum_{n=1}^{2} w_{mn} \sum_{i=1}^{3}(w_{C_i} d_E(W^i_{C_i,m,n}, W^q_{C_i,m,n}))$, where $W_{C_i,1,1}$ and $W_{C_i,1,2}, W_{C_i,2,1}, W_{C_i,2,2}$ denotes the 8×8 upper left corner and, respectively, the three surrounding 8×8 submatrices of W_{C_i}, and with d_E the Euclidean distance. By raising w_{C_2} or w_{C_3} the importance of color variation in the image is emphasized, while raising

$w_{2,1}, w_{1,2}$ or $w_{2,2}$ the vertical, horizontal, or diagonal edge details in the image are emphasized.

Result presentation. The first few matches are presented in decreasing similarity order.

Applications. The system is used at Stanford University Library to assist teaching and research projects in liberal art departments.

		ADL	AMORE	ASSERT	BDLP	Blobworld	CANDID	C-bird	CBVQ	Chabot	CHROMA	DrawSearch	FIDS	FIR	FOCUS	ImageRETRO
Keywords		★	★		★					★						
Face Detection																
Layout				★		★		★			★		★		★	
Shape	Other							★[4]								★[6]
	Elementary descriptors			★		★		★	★						★	
	Bounding box/ellipse															
	Elastic models															
	Fourier descriptors											★				
	Template matching		★													
	Edge direction histogram															
Texture	Other															
	Edge statistics			★				★					★			
	Local binary patterns												★			
	Random fields											★				
	Atomic texture features			★		★	★									
	Wavelet, Gabor, Fourier	★							★				★	★		
Color	Other				★[2]			★[3]								★[5]
	Dominant colors		★				★	★			★					
	Region histogram			★		★										
	Color coherence vector															
	Color moments			★								★				★
	Correllation histogram															
	Global/subimage histogram							★	★	★			★		★	★
	Eigen image															
System		ADL	AMORE	ASSERT	BDLP	Blobworld	CANDID	C-bird	CBVQ	Chabot	CHROMA	DrawSearch	FIDS	FIR	FOCUS	ImageRETRO

ImageRover		★								★			★									★		★
ImageScape							★	★[7]		★		★					★			★		★	★	
JACOB		★								★			★											
LCPD												★		★[8]										
MARS		★							★	★							★					★		★
MetaSEEk		★								★														★
MIR		★	★																			★	★	★
NETRA						★			★								★					★		
Photobook	★										★							★					★	
Picasso						★												★	★	★		★		
PicHunter		★	★		★																			★
PicSOM				★										★[1]	★		★					★		
PicToSeek		★																			★[9]			
QBIC		★		★						★						★				★		★		★
Quicklook		★	★	★	★			★[10]	★	★			★		★					★		★		
Shoebox				★				★[11]																★
SIMBA														★[12]										
SMURF		★																			★[13]			
SQUID																					★[16]			
Surfimage	★	★							★	★				★[14]	★			★						
SYNAPSE														★[15]										
TODAI													★											★
VIR																								★
VisualSEEk							★												★	★		★		

WebSEEk		★																						★
WebSeer		★						★[17]															★	★
WISE									★															

1 local probability
3 DCT of chromaticity
5 greyness, background proportion
7 Laplacian
9 angles between edges, and cross ratios of them
11 color channel variance
13 weighted point sets, polylines
15 multiscale intensity surface derivatives
17 farthest neighbor histogram

2 number of regions with that color
4 generalized Hough transform
6 number of regions, number of holes
8 projection histogram
10 spatial chromaticity histogram
12 histogram of polynomial of local intensities
14 intensity surface curvature histogram
16 curvature scale space

Table 5.1. Overview of systems and their search features.

4. Summary and Conclusions

The features used in the systems discussed in this chapter are listed in Table 5.1. The features are classified into the low level classes color, texture, and shape, and the higher level classes layout and face detection. The use of keywords is also listed.

We have tried to group the low level features into meaningful categories. For example, various forms of choosing important colors are grouped into 'dominant colors'. The 'eigen image' is listed under color, because it is a feature derived from the global image color values, rather than local patterns as in texture. The 'atomic texture features' are features such as contrast, anisotropy, density, randomness, directionality, softness, and uniformity, often variations of the Tamura features [169], and often derived from a co-occurrence matrix of pixel values. The 'edge statistics' include the edge image histogram, edge orientation histogram, and others. Recall that we consider edge orientation over all pixels as texture, but edge orientation at only region contours as shape information, see section 2. The 'elementary shape descriptors' are features such as centroid, area, major axis orientation, eccentricity, circularity, and features derived from algebraic moments. The feature 'layout' is the absolute or relative spatial position of the color, texture, or shape features. Taking color histograms per fixed subimage is a simple way of exploiting spatial layout; considering the relative position (constellation) of regions is more complex.

Of the 42 systems in the table, 33 use any kind of color features, 25 use texture, 21 use shape, 16 layout, and 4 use face detection. Perhaps the reason for this order of frequencies of usage is their complexity and, coupled to that, effectiveness. The simpler the features can be extracted, the easier it is to implement it in the system, and the easier it is to use that feature class in the right way. For example, color features are often found effective, because good color features are not very difficult to design and implement. However, shape features that are for example robust against noise and occlusion, are more involved. As a result, only overly simple features such as area are used, which is often little effective.

Most systems are products of research, and therefore emphasize one aspect of content-based retrieval. Sometimes this is the sketching capability in the user interface, sometimes it is the new indexing data structure, etc. Some systems exist in a research version and in a commercial or production version. The commercial version is usually less advanced, and shows more standard searching capabilities.

A number of systems provide a user interface that allows more powerful query formulation than is useful in the demo system. For example, if a user can paint a cartoon, but the database contains only airplanes, the system will always retrieve images of airplanes. For such a limited database, no powerful sketching interface is needed. Also, because most workstations have a mouse, but easy sketching needs a pencil, such a painting tool is often of little use. Drawing polygonal shapes with a mouse works well, however.

Most systems use color and texture features, few systems use shape feature, and still less use layout features. The retrieval on color usually yield images with similar colors. Retrieval on texture does not always yield images that have clearly the same texture, unless the database contains many images with a dominant texture. Searching on shape gives often surprising results. Apparently the shape features used for matching are not the most effective ones.

Indexing data structures are often not used. Indeed, for small collections of images, an indexing data structure is not needed, and a linear search can be sufficiently fast. Contemporary computers can perform simple matching of hundreds of images in near real time.

It is difficult to evaluate how successful content-based image retrieval systems are, in terms of effectiveness, efficiency, and flexibility. Of course there are the notions of precision (the ratio of relevant images to the total number of images retrieved) and recall (the percentage of relevant images among all possible relevant images). Many articles about systems give figures about precision and recall. Most of them are good, but hard to verify. One reason is that many hyperlinks on the Web are not active anymore, a design flaw of the Web. However, there are also considerations intrinsic to retrieval systems.

If the database only contains fighting airplanes, and the user can only ask for images similar to a chosen fighting airplanes, the system will successfully return fighting airplanes. If the domain is so narrow, it may make more sense to look for dissimilar images than for similar images. On the other hand, if the database is very diverse and contains only a single image of a chicken, asking for images similar to that chicken will not result in other chicken images. The larger the collection of images, the more chance that it contains an image similar to the query image. The Web is a large enough test set, and free of charge, reason why some image retrieval systems exploit webcrawlers. Having a specific object in mind, looking for images with similar objects is a frustrating experience, however. Indeed, before you learn to walk, you crawl first.

It is widely recognized that most current content-based image retrieval systems work with low level features (color, texture, shape), and that next generation systems should operate at a higher semantic level. One way to achieve this is to let the system recognize objects and scenes. Although this is difficult in general, it should be feasible for specific domains. For example, body plans have been used to recognize animals and people [57]. Once separate entities in images are recognized, the way to semantic reasoning lies open.

Chapter 6

CASE STUDY: MUSE

In this chapter we present **MUSE** (**MU**ltimedia **SE**arch and Retrieval Using Relevance Feedback), a CBVIR system with relevance feedback and learning capabilities developed by the authors over the past two years. MUSE is an ongoing project within the Department of Computer Science and Engineering at Florida Atlantic University. The ultimate goal of this project is to build an intelligent system for searching and retrieving visual information in large repositories[1].

1. Overview of the System

MUSE works under a purely content-based visual information retrieval paradigm. No additional information (metadata) is used during any stage. The current prototype supports several browsing, searching, and retrieval modes (described in more detail in Section 2). From a research perspective, the most important operating modes are the ones that employ relevance feedback (with or without clustering).

Within MUSE we have proposed and implemented two distinct and completely independent models for solving the image retrieval problem without resorting to metadata and including the user in the loop. The first model — which will be henceforth referred to as **RF (Relevance Feedback)** — implements an extension of the model originally proposed by Cox et al.[45]. It uses a compact color-based feature vector obtained by partitioning the HSV color space into 12 segments — each of which maps onto a semantic color — and counting the number of pixels in an

[1]MUSE is a work in progress and the information presented in this chapter may be subject to frequent updates. Please contact the authors if you need the latest information on the status of the project.

image that fall in each segment, plus the global information of average brightness and saturation in the image. It employs a Bayesian learning algorithm which updates the probability of each image in the database being the target based on the user's actions (labeling an image as good, bad, or indifferent).

The second model — which will be henceforth referred to as **RFC (Relevance Feedback with Clustering)** — uses a general-purpose clustering algorithm, PAM (Partitioning Around Medoids) [91] — or its variant for large databases, CLARA (Clustering LARge Applications) [91] — and a combination of color-, texture-, and edge(shape)-based features. Each feature vector is extracted independently and applied to the input of the clustering algorithm. This model uses novel (heuristic) approaches to displaying images and updating probabilities that are strongly dependent on the quality of the clustering structure obtained by the chosen clustering algorithm.

Both models assume that the search and retrieval process should be based solely on image contents automatically extracted during the (off-line) feature extraction stage. Moreover, they strive at reducing the burden on the user's side as much as possible, limiting the user's actions to few mouse clicks, and hiding the complexity of the underlying search and retrieval engine from the end user.

Figure 6.1 shows the main components of MUSE in "Relevance Feedback with Clustering" (RFC) mode. Part of the system's operations happen off-line while some actions are executed online. The off-line stage includes feature extraction, representation, and organization for each image in the archive. The online interactions are commanded by the user through the GUI. The relevant (*good* or *bad*) images selected by the user have their characteristics compared against the other images in the database. The result of the similarity comparison is the update and ranking of each image's probability of being the target image. Based on them, the system stores learning information and decides on which candidate images to display next. After a few iterations, the target image should be among those displayed on screen, i.e., the search should have converged towards the desired target.

2. The User's Perspective

MUSE's interface is simple, clear, and intuitive. It contains a menu, two toolbars and a working area divided in two parts: the left-hand side contains a selected image (optional) and the right-hand side works as a browser, whose details depend on the operation mode. The latest prototype of MUSE supports six operation modes:

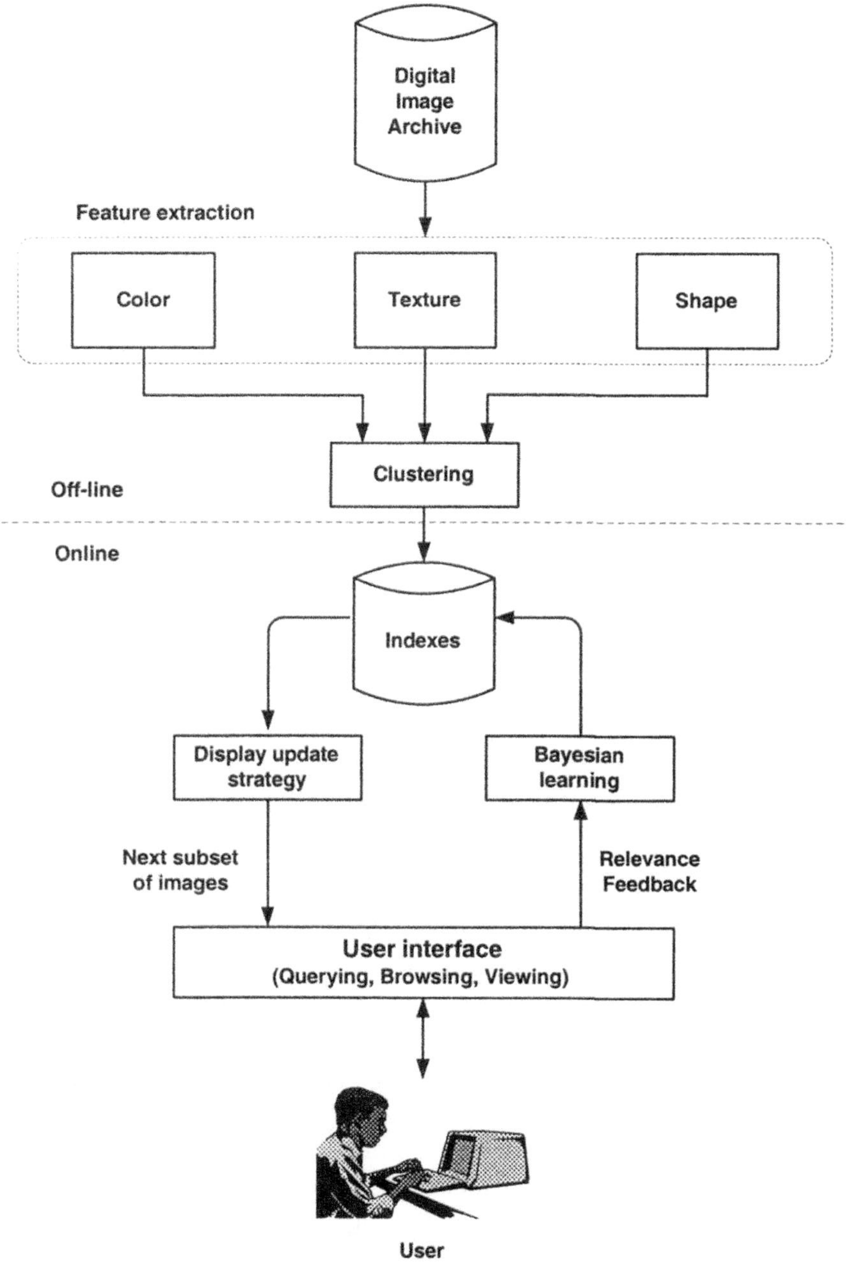

Figure 6.1. MUSE: block diagram.

1 free browsing,

2 random ("slot machine") browsing,

3 query-by-example (QBE),

4 relevance feedback (RF),

5 relevance feedback with clustering (RFC), and

6 cluster browsing.

In the free browsing mode (Figure 6.2), the browser shows thumbnail versions of the images in the currently selected directory. The random browsing mode (Figure 6.3) shuffles the directory contents before showing the reduced-size version of its images, working as a baseline against which the fourth and fifth modes (RF and RFC) can be compared. The query-by-example mode (Figure 6.4) has been implemented to serve as a testbed for the feature extraction and similarity measurement stages. Using an image (left) as an example, the best matches (along with their dissimilarity values) are shown in the browser area. Finally, the cluster browsing mode (Figure 6.5[2]) provides a convenient way to visually inspect the results of the clustering algorithm, i.e., which images have been assigned to which clusters.

The RF and RFC modes look alike from the user's point of view, despite using different features and algorithms. Both modes start from a subset of images and refine their understanding of which image is the target based on the user input (specifying each image as *good*, *bad*, or neither). Let us assume a session in which the user is searching for an image of the Canadian flag, using the RF mode. The user would initially see a subset of nine[3] images on the browser side (Figure 6.6). Based on how similar or dissimilar each image is when compared to the desired target image, the user can select zero or more of the currently displayed images as *good* or *bad* examples before pressing the *Go* button. The *Select* button associated with each image changes its color to green — with a left-click (when the image has been chosen as a good example) — or red — with a right-click (when the image has been chosen as a bad example). Selecting relevant images and pressing the *Go* button are the only required user actions. Upon detecting that the *Go* button has been pressed, MUSE first verifies if one or more images have been selected. If

[2]The first five images — with clear predominance of red — belong to a cluster, while the last four — with lots of yellow — belong to another cluster.

[3]The number of images displayed on the browser area can be configured by the user. Current options are four, nine, or 25.

Figure 6.2. MUSE: free browsing mode.

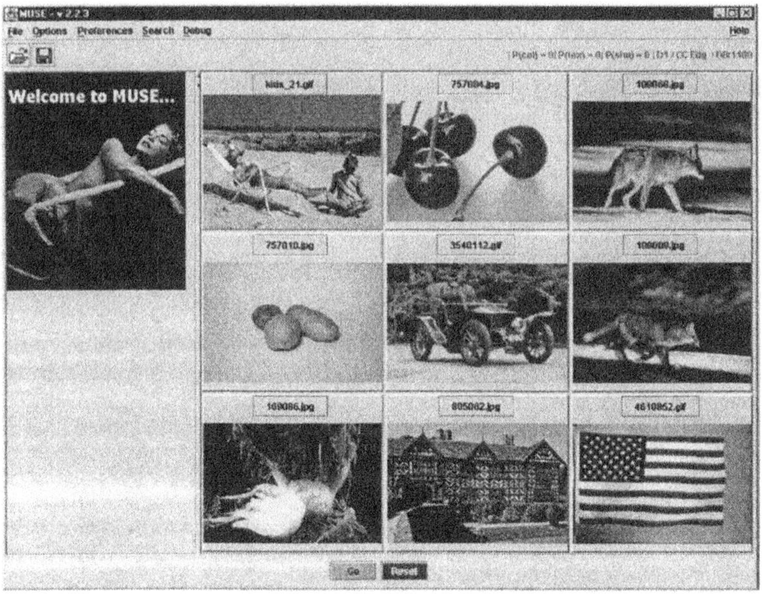

Figure 6.3. MUSE: random ("slot machine") browsing mode.

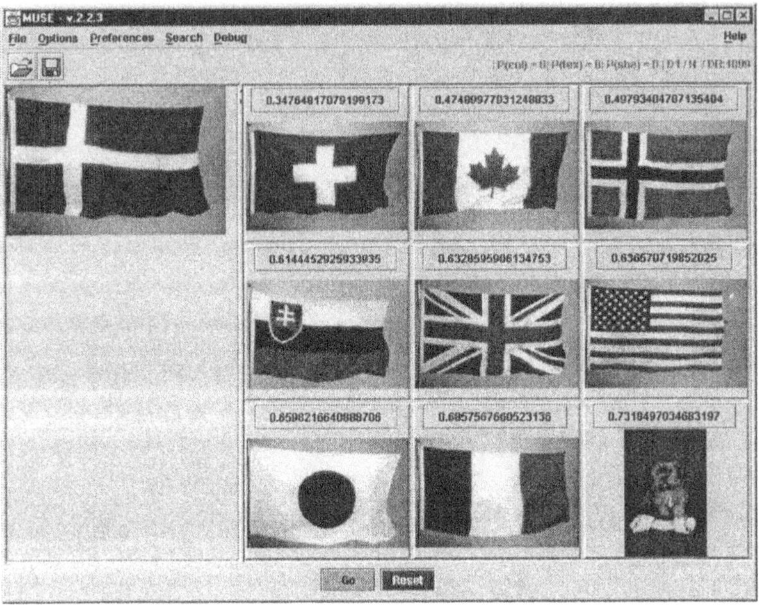

Figure 6.4. MUSE: query-by-example mode, using color only.

Figure 6.5. MUSE: cluster browsing mode.

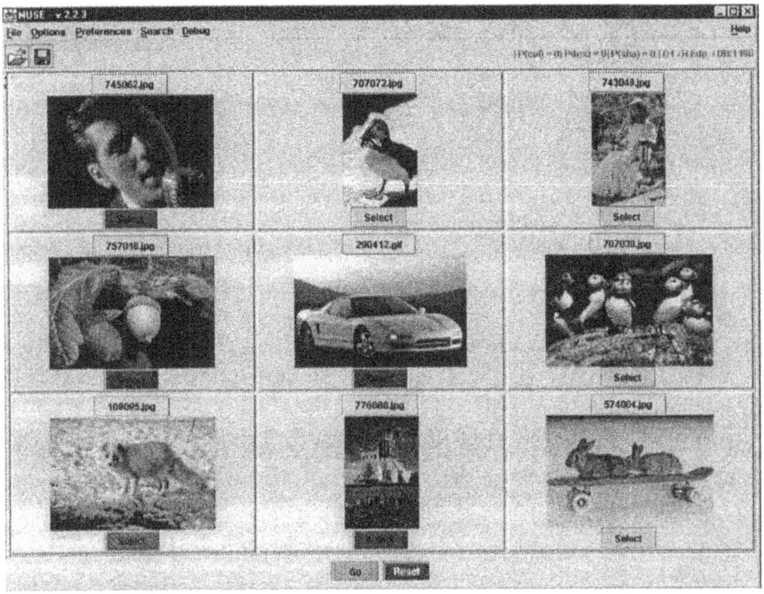

Figure 6.6. MUSE: relevance feedback mode: initial screen. [4]

so, it recalculates the probabilities of each image being the target image and displays a new subset of images that should be closer to the target than the ones displayed so far. If the user has not selected any image, the system displays a new subset of images selected at random. After a few additional iterations — only one in this case (Figure 6.7) — the system eventually converges to the target image (Figure 6.8).

3. The RF Mode

The first proposed model for image retrieval using relevance feedback uses a simple set of color-based features and a probabilistic model of information retrieval based on image similarity.

3.1 Features

Color is the only feature used by MUSE when operating in RF mode. Color information is extracted by first converting the RGB representa-

[4]The image display area has been collapsed in this sequence of figures for better visualization. The top-left, middle-left, center, and bottom-center images were labeled as *bad*, while the bottom-left was labeled as *good*, because of the amount of white it contains.

[5]The bottom-left and bottom-center images were labeled as *good*, while all the others were labeled as *bad*.

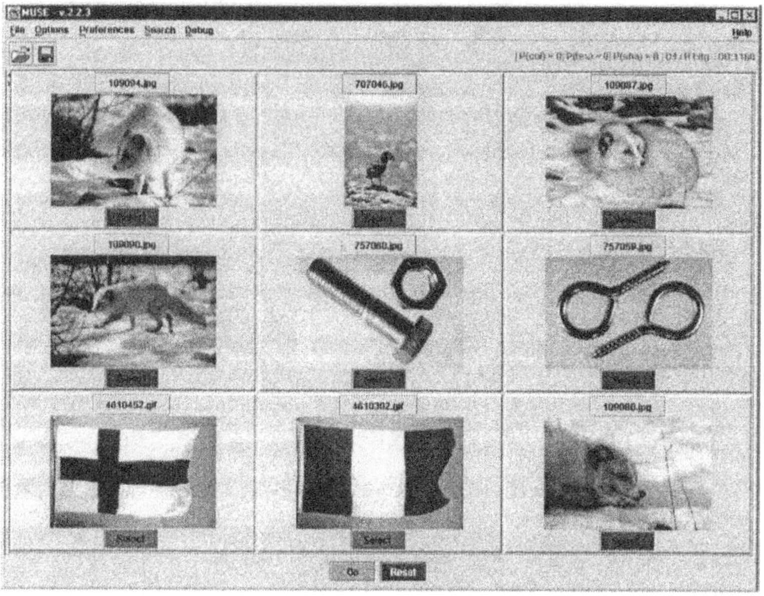

Figure 6.7. MUSE: relevance feedback mode: second iteration[5].

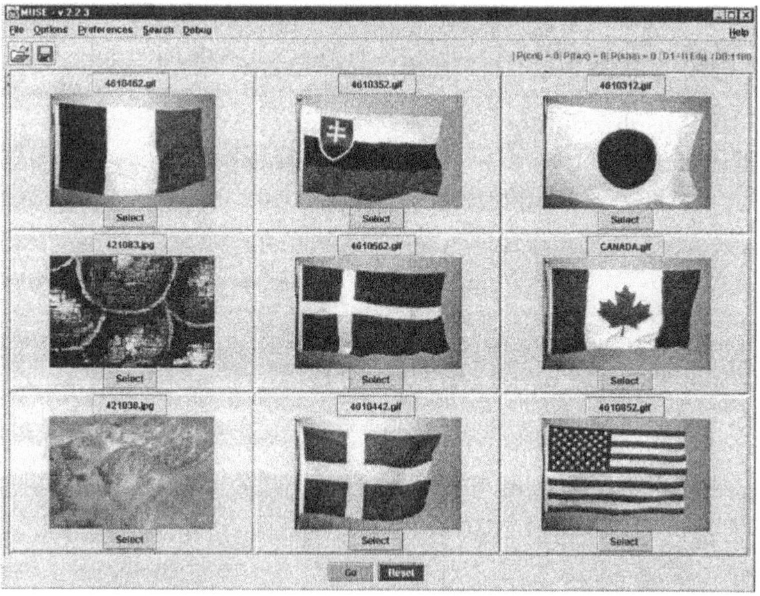

Figure 6.8. MUSE: relevance feedback mode: target image (middle row – right column) found on third iteration.

Table 6.1. Color-based feature set.

Color	$H(°)$	$S(\%)$	$V(\%)$	*Weight*
Pink	-40...+30	5...40	10...100	0.0847
Brown	-50...+80	2...70	2...40	0.0524
Yellow	20...80	10...100	8...100	0.0524
Orange	15...50	10...100	2...100	0.1532
Red	-40...+30	40...100	10...100	0.1129
Green	70...170	10...100	3...100	0.0363
Blue	170...260	2...100	3...100	0.1089
Purple (magenta)	260...340	10...100	3...100	0.2016
Black	0...360	0...100	0...3	0.1169
Gray	0...360	0...15	3...90	0.0605
White	0...360	0...15	80...100	0.0202

tion of each image into its HSV equivalent — which is more suitable to partitioning according to the semantic meaning of each color — and their mapping to regions in the HSV space. Then, the HSV space is partitioned into 12 segments, whose values of H, S, and V are shown in Table 6.1[6]. Each of these segments corresponds to a color and is assigned a weight for the similarity measurement phase. The assignment of a semantic meaning (a well-known color) to each segment was based on the literature on color theory [146]. The mapping between each color and the corresponding interval values of H, S, and V was refined by experiments with synthetic test images created by the authors. The weights assigned to each color have been adapted from [43]. The normalized amounts of each color in the image constitute that image's feature vector.

3.2 Probabilistic Model

MUSE is based on a Bayesian framework for relevance feedback proposed by Cox and colleagues [45]. It is assumed that a user is looking for a specific image in the database (the "target testing" paradigm [43]) by means of a series of display / action iterations. The database images will be denoted $T_1, \ldots, T_n$. Unless otherwise noted, MUSE will assume that the desired image, henceforth called *target image*, is in the database.

During each iteration t = 1, 2, ... of a MUSE session, the system displays a subset D_t of N images[7] from its database and the user takes

[6]The 12th segment is not associated with any color. It is used as a catch-all case for pixels that do not fit into any other segment.
[7]The value of N can be selected by the user and is typically four or nine.

an action A_t in response, which the system observes. Possible user's actions are: labeling each image within D_t as *good*, *bad*, or leaving it unlabeled (*indifferent*).

D_t can be represented as:

$$D_t = (x_1(r_1), \ldots, x_N(r_N)) \tag{6.1}$$

where: $x_k(r_k)$ is a particular image $(T_1, \ldots, T_n)$ given rating r,

$$r = \begin{cases} g & \text{if} \quad \textbf{image rated ``good''} \\ b & \text{if} \quad \textbf{image rated ``bad''} \\ i & \text{if} \quad \textbf{image rated ``indifferent''} \end{cases}$$

and k is an indicator of the image's position on screen.

The history H_t of the session through iteration t will consist of the sequence of images selected at each iteration up to and including t and associated ratings r:

$H_t = \{D_1, D_2, \ldots D_t\}$, where D_1 is selected at random and successive values of D are dependent on the user's previous actions.

After each iteration t MUSE recalculates the probability that a particular image T_i is the user's target T, given the session history, for all values of i, $1 \leq i \leq n$. This probability is denoted $P(T_i = T|H_t)$. The system's estimate before starting the session, i.e., the *a priori* probability that a particular image T_i is the target, is denoted as $P(T_i = T)$. After iteration t the system must select the next set D_{t+1} of images to display[8]. From Bayes's rule we have:

$$P(T_i = T|H_t) = \frac{P(H_t|T_i = T)P(T_i = T)}{\sum_{j=1}^{n} P(H_t|T_j = T)P(T_j = T)} \tag{6.2}$$

In other words, the *a posteriori* probability that image T_i is the target, given the observed history, may be computed by evaluating $P(H_t|T_i = T)$, which is the history's likelihood given that the target is, in fact, T_i. MUSE initially assigns the *a priori* probability $P(T_i = T) = 1/n$ $(i = 1, 2, \ldots, n)$ to each image at the beginning of each session.

The probabilistic model used in MUSE is a variant of the one proposed by Cox et al. [45]. MUSE gives the user three levels of action upon each displayed image: labeling the image as *good*, *bad*, or not labeling it (*indifferent*), while Cox et al.'s model works with only two levels: *good* and *indifferent*.

[8] In RF mode this is done by selecting the most likely images. An alternative display strategy has been proposed and implemented as part of the RFC mode and will be described in the next section.

In our model (MUSE):

- T is the target image
- D_t is the subset of images displayed during each iteration t
- $x_k(r_k)$ is a particular image displayed at screen position k during an iteration
- $\mathcal{F}$ is a set of real-valued functions corresponding to the computed features of the images, i.e., the feature vector for that image. The size of the feature vector, $\|\mathcal{F}\|$, will be denoted α. In RF mode[9] $\alpha = 14$.
- W_f is the weight of a particular feature, $f \in \mathcal{F}$, within the feature vector
- $V(T_i, T_j)$ is the "similarity score" between two images, T_i and T_j, $i, j \leq n$, $i \neq j$.

During each iteration t the system calculates the similarity score $V(T_i, x_k)$ between each displayed image (regardless of its ranking by the user) x_k, where k is the image's position on the screen, $1 \leq k \leq N$, and each (hypothesized target) image in the database T_i using equations 6.3 and 6.4.

$$V(T_i, x_k) = \sum_{j=1}^{\alpha} W_f \sum_{m=1}^{N} c_k(m, j) \tag{6.3}$$

where

$$c_k(m, j) = \begin{cases} 1 & \text{if} \quad d(T_i, x_k) < d(T_i, x_m) \\ 0.5 & \text{if} \quad d(T_i, x_k) = d(T_i, x_m) \\ 0 & \text{if} \quad d(T_i, x_k) > d(T_i, x_m) \end{cases}$$

where $1 \leq m \leq N, k \neq m$, and $d(T_i, x_k)$ is a distance measure, in our case, the L_1 norm:

$$d(T_i, x_k) = |f_j(T_i) - f_j(x_k)| \tag{6.4}$$

The values of $V(T_i, x_k)$, or simply V, are normalized to a value $P(T_i, x_k)$, or simply P, in the $[0, 1]$ range using the sigmoid function given by equation 6.5:

$$P = \frac{1}{1 + \frac{e^{(M-V)}}{\sigma}} \tag{6.5}$$

[9] In the beginning, the feature vector had 12 elements. Some time later two additional features — average brightness and average saturation — were added, turning it into a 14-element feature vector.

```
if (first iteration) {
    Initialize each image's probability, P(Ti=T) = 1/n,
    where 'n' is the number of image files in the database.

    Display D randomly selected images from the database.
}
else {
    UpdateProbabilities();

    Display the D images with the highest probabilities.
}
```

Figure 6.9. Pseudocode for the RF mode.

where

M and σ were empirically determined[10] as a function of the feature vector and the total number n of images in the database. In our current implementation, $M = 0.4n$ and $\sigma = 0.18n$.

Finally, the estimated probability $P(T_i = T|H_t)$ that a particular image T_i is the target, given the images displayed so far and how they were rated, which will be called $S(i)$, $(i = 1, 2, \ldots, n)$, is computed as a function of the value of $P(T_i, x_k)$ and the information provided by the user of whether the image was good, bad, or irrelevant, using equation 6.6.

$$S(i) = \prod_{k=1, r_k=g}^{k=N} P(T_i, x_k) \times \prod_{k=1, r_k=b}^{k=N} (1 - P(T_i, x_k)) \tag{6.6}$$

The values of S for all images in the database are then normalized so that they add up to 1. Images are then ranked according to their current probability of being the target and the best N images are displayed back to the user.

The pseudocode for the general Bayesian relevance feedback algorithm is presented in Figure 6.9. The key function is **UpdateProbabilities**(), whose pseudocode is shown in Figure 6.10. **CalculateS**(Ti) (Figure 6.11) is the function that updates the probability of each image being the target based on the good and bad examples selected by the user.

[10]Using a spreadsheet and evaluating the "goodness" of the resulting curve for several combinations of M and σ.

```
UpdateProbabilities() {
    for (all displayed images)
        Reset the probability of the current image to 0.

    for (each image Ti in the database)
    {
        /* Update P(Ti=T) taking the user behavior function
        into account*/
        P(Ti=T) = P(Ti=T) * CalculateS(Ti);

        /* Normalize P(T=Ti) */
        P(Ti=T) = P(Ti=T) / sum(P(Ti=T))
    }
}
```

Figure 6.10. Pseudocode for the **UpdateProbabilities**() function.

4. The RFC Mode

Despite the good numerical results reported by the system under the RF mode (see Section 5.1), it was further improved in a number of ways:

1 **Increase the number and diversity of features.** The RF mode relied only on color information and encoded this knowledge in a fairly compact 12-element feature vector. It was decided to investigate and test alternative algorithms for extraction of color, texture, shape (edges), and color layout information.

2 **Use clustering techniques to group together semantically similar images.** It was decided to investigate and test clustering algorithms and their suitability to the content-based image retrieval problem.

3 **Redesign the learning algorithm to work with clusters.** As a consequence of the anticipated use of clustering algorithms, an alternative learning algorithm was developed. The new algorithm preserves the Bayesian nature of the RF mode, but updates the scores of each cluster — rather than individual images — at each iteration.

4 **Improve the display update strategy.** The RF mode used a simple, greedy approach to displaying the next best candidates, selecting the images with largest probabilities, which sometimes leaves the user with limited options. An alternative algorithm was proposed, whose details are described later in this chapter.

```
CalculateS(Ti) {
    S = 1.0;

    for (each displayed image xk(rk) in D)
    {
        V = 0.0;
        for (each feature f in F)
            for (each xq(rq) in D, xq(rq) != xk(rk))
            {
                if (abs(f(Ti) - f(xk(rk))) <
                    abs (f(Ti) - f(xq(rq))))
                        V = V + Wf;
                else if (abs(f(Ti) - f(xk(rk))) ==
                         abs (f(Ti) - f(xq(rq))))
                        V = V + 0.5*Wf;
            }

        P = 1.0 / (1.0 + exp((M-V)/sigma));
        if (rk == g)
        /* if the user selected D(i) as a good example */
            S = S * P;
        else if (rk == b)
        /* if the user selected D(i) as a bad example */
            S = S * (1 - P);
        else
            /* do nothing */
    }
    return(S);
}
```

Figure 6.11. Pseudocode for the **CalculateS**(Ti) function.

All these improvements — described in more detail in Subsections 4.1 through 4.4 — should not overrule the basic assumptions about the way the user interacts with the system. In other words, however tempting it might be, it was decided that the amount of burden on the users' side should not increase for the sake of helping the system better understand their preferences.

4.1 More and Better Features

The RF mode relied on a color-based 12-element feature vector[11]. It did not contain any information on texture, shape, or color-spatial relationships within the images. Moreover, the partition of the HSV space into regions that map semantically meaningful colors, although based on the literature on color perception and refined by testing, was nevertheless arbitrary and rigid: a pixel with H = 30°, S = 10%, and V = 50%, would be labeled as "pink", while another slightly different pixel, with H = 31°, S = 10%, and V = 50%, would be labeled as "brown" and fall into a different bin.

We studied and implemented the following improvements to the feature vector:

- **Color histogram**[165] (with and without the simple color normalization algorithm described in [166]). The implementation was tested under QBE mode and the quality of the results convinced us to replace the original color-based 14-element feature vector by a 64-bin RGB color histogram.

- **Color correlogram.** The main limitation of the color histogram approach is its inability to distinguish images whose color distribution is identical, but whose pixels are organized according to a different layout. The color correlogram — a feature originally proposed by Huang [86] — overcomes this limitation by encoding color-spatial information into (a collection of) co-occurrence matrices. We implemented a 64-bin color autocorrelogram for 4 different distance values (which results in a 256-element feature vector) as an alternative to color histograms. It was tested under the QBE mode, but the results were not convincing enough to make it the color-based feature of choice.

- **Texture features.** We built a 20-element feature vector using the variance of the gray level co-occurrence matrix for five distances (d) and four different orientations (θ) as a measure of the texture properties of an image, as suggested in [7][12]. For each combination of d and θ, the variance $v(d,\theta)$ of gray level spatial dependencies within the image is given by:

$$v(d,\theta) = \sum_{i=0}^{L-1} \sum_{j=0}^{L-1} (i-j)^2 P(i,j;d,\theta) \tag{6.7}$$

[11]Some time later it was decided to add two more features — average brightness and average saturation — turning it into a 14-element feature vector, referred to as HSV+.

[12]This feature is a difference moment of P that measures the contrast in the image. Rosenfeld [134] called this feature the *moment of inertia*.

where: L is the number of gray levels, and $P(i, j; d, \theta)$ is the probability that two neighboring pixels (one with gray level i and the other with gray level j) separated by distance d at orientation θ occur in the image. Experiments with the texture feature vector revealed limited usefulness when the image repositories are general and unconstrained.

- **Edge-based shape features.** To convey the information about shape without resorting to segmenting the image into meaningful objects and background, we adopted a very simple set of descriptors: a normalized count of the number of edge pixels obtained by applying the Sobel edge-detection operators in eight different directions (0°, 45°, 90°, 135°, 180°, 225°, 270°, and 315°) and thresholding the results. Despite its simplicity, the edge-based shape descriptor performed fairly well when combined with color histogram (with or without color constancy).

4.2 Clustering

The proposed clustering strategy uses a well-known clustering algorithm, PAM (Partitioning Around Medoids) [91], applied to each feature vector separately, resulting in a partition of the database into K_1 (color-based) + K_2 (texture-based) + K_3 (shape-based) clusters (Figure 6.12). At the end of the clustering stage each image T_i in the database maps onto a triple $\{c_1, c_2, c_3\}$, where c_j indicates to which cluster the image belongs to according to color ($j = 1$), texture ($j = 2$), or shape ($j = 3$), and $1 \leq c_1 \leq K_1$, $1 \leq c_2 \leq K_2$, and $1 \leq c_3 \leq K_3$.

The clustering structure obtained for each individual feature is used as an input by a learning algorithm that updates the probabilities of each feature (which gives a measure of its relevance for that particular session) and the probability of each cluster, based on the user information on which images are good or bad. The main algorithm's pseudocode is shown in Figure 6.13. The pseudocode for the **DisplayFirstSetOfImages**() function is presented in Figure 6.14. The pseudocode for the **UpdateProbabilities**() function is shown in Figure 6.15. Finally[13], the pseudocode for **UpdatePf**(), called by **UpdateProbabilities()** is presented in Figure 6.16.

From a visual perception point of view, our algorithm infers relevance information about each feature without requiring the user to explicitly do so. In other words, it starts by assigning each feature a normalized relevance score. During each iteration, based on the clusters where the

[13]The pseudocode for the **DisplayNextBestImages**() function will be presented later in this chapter.

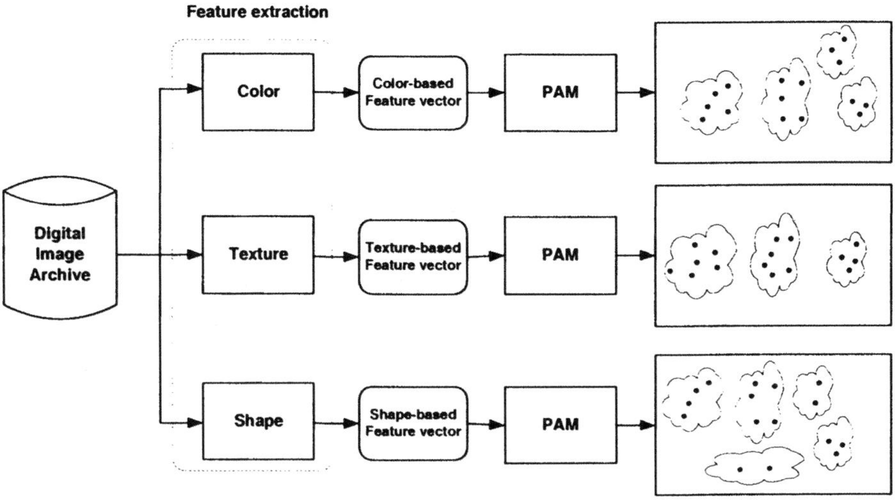

Figure 6.12. The clustering concept for three different features: color, texture, and shape. In this case, $K_1 = 4$, $K_2 = 3$, and $K_3 = 5$.

good and bad examples come from, the importance of each feature is dynamically updated.

In terms of computational cost, it no longer updates the probability of each *image* being a target, but it updates the probability of each *cluster* containing the desired target, instead. This reduces the cost of updating probabilities at each iteration from $O(N^2 n\alpha)$ (in the RF mode) to $O(NC\beta)$ (in the RFC mode), where: N is the number of images displayed at each iteration, n is the size of the database, $\alpha = \| \mathcal{F} \|$ is the size of the feature vector ($\alpha = 14$ in the RF mode), C is the total number of clusters, and β is the number of features being considered ($\beta = 3$ in the RFC mode). Since $C << n$, and $\beta < \alpha$, the increase in speed is evident.

The choice of the values of K_1, K_2, and K_3 is based on the *silhouette coefficient* [91], a figure of merit that measures the amount of clustering structure found by the clustering algorithm.

4.3 Learning

The current implementation of MUSE uses a Bayesian learning method in which each observed image labeled as *good* or *bad* incrementally decreases or increases the probability that a hypothesis is correct. The main difference between the previous and the current learning algorithms is that in the RF mode, at each iteration, we update the probability of

```
Apply the PAM clustering algorithm to each feature vector
separately. (The result will be a partition of the database
according to: color (K1 clusters) and/or texture (K2
clusters) and/or shape (K3 clusters)).

if (first iteration) {
    Initialize each image's probability, P(i) = 1/n, where
    n is the number of image files in the database.

    Initialize each cluster's probability, P(cg), as the sum
    of the probabilities of the images that belong to it.

    Initialize each feature's probability, P(g) = 1/G, where
    G is the total number of features being considered.

    DisplayFirstSetOfImages();
} else {
    UpdateProbabilities();

    DisplayNextBestImages();
}
```

Figure 6.13. Pseudocode for the RFC mode.

```
DisplayFirstSetOfImages() {

    Sort the K1 color-based clusters according to their
    size.

    Choose one representative image from each cluster,
    starting with the largest.

    If the selected number of images per iteration is
    greater than the number of clusters, select another
    representative image from each  cluster, and so on,
    until all browser positions have been filled out.
}
```

Figure 6.14. Pseudocode for the **DisplayFirstSetOfImages()** function.

```
UpdateProbabilities() {
    for (all displayed images)
    {
        if (image was labeled as "good")
            for (all features g)
                P(cg|g) = 2*P(cg|g)
                /* double the probability
                of the clusters to which it belongs */

        if (image was labeled as "bad")
            for (all features g)}
                P(cg|g) = 0.5*P(cg|g)
                /* reduce the probability of the clusters
                to which it belongs to half of
                their original value */

        Reset the probability of the current image to 0.
    }

    /* nGood = number of images labeled by the user
               as "good"
       nBad = number of images labeled by the user
              as "bad" */

    if (nGood == 0 && nBad >= 2)
        UpdatePf("bad");

    if (nBad == 0 && nGood >= 2)
        UpdatePf("good");

    if (nBad == 0 && nGood == 0)
        /* do nothing */

    if (nBad != 0 && nGood != 0)
        UpdatePf("both");

    Normalize all values of P(g) and P(cg|g).
}
```

Figure 6.15. Pseudocode for the **UpdateProbabilities**() function.

```
UpdatePf(mode) {
    if (mode == "good" OR mode == "bad")
        for (all pairs of both good or both bad examples
              (i,j))
            for (all features g)
                if (i and j belong to different clusters
                                              according to g)
                    P(g) = 0.5*P(g);
                else
                    P(g) = 2*P(g);

    else /* mode = "both" */
        for (all pairs of good (i) and bad (j) examples)
            for (all features g)
                if (i and j belong to different clusters
                                              according to g)
                    P(g) = 2*P(g);
                else
                    P(g) = 0.5*P(g);
}
```

Figure 6.16. Pseudocode for the **UpdatePf()** function.

each *image* being the target, while in the second prototype we update the probability of each *cluster* to which an image belongs. By doing so, we reduce the computational cost of the probability update routines — sometimes at the expense of the quality of the results, which will be proportional to the quality of the cluster structure produced by the clustering algorithm. This approach lends itself naturally to the *similarity testing* (as opposed to *target testing*) paradigm, in which the user would stop whenever an image close to what she had in mind is found. Since similar images should belong to the same cluster, the algorithm naturally produces meaningful results — again, depending on how good was the clustering structure — under the new paradigm, too.

Here is a formal description of our learning algorithm. In this algorithm:

- $P(T_i = T)$ is the probability that a particular image T_i is the desired target, $1 \leq i \leq n$, where n is the size of the database.

- $P(T_i|C_{gj})$ is the conditional probability that the target image belongs to cluster j assuming that the images were clustered according to feature $g \in \mathcal{G}$, where $\mathcal{G} = \{col, tex, sha\}$ is the feature set.
- $P(C_{gj}|g)$ is the conditional probability of a particular cluster C_{gj} given the feature $g \in \mathcal{G}$ according to which the cluster was obtained.
- $P(g)$ is the probability that feature g is relevant for a particular session.

According to the law of total probability:

$$P(T_i = T) = \sum_{j=1}^{C} \sum_{g=1}^{\beta} P(T_i|C_{gj})P(C_{gj}|g)P(g) \tag{6.8}$$

where

$$C = K_1 + K_2 + K_3 \tag{6.9}$$

is the total number of clusters.

Since an image can only belong to one cluster under a certain feature, $P(T_i|C_{gj}) = 0$ for all values of j except one, w, where $w \in \{c_1, c_2, c_3\}$ is the cluster to which it belongs under that particular feature.

We can rewrite Equation 6.8 as:

$$\begin{aligned} P(T_i = T) &= \sum_{g=1}^{\beta} P(T_i|C_{gw})P(C_{gj}|g)P(g), && (6.10) \\ &= P(T_i|C_{col\,c_1})P(C_{col\,c_1}|g)P(g) + \\ &\quad P(T_i|C_{tex\,c_2})P(C_{tex\,c_2}|g)P(g) + \\ &\quad P(T_i|C_{sha\,c_3})P(C_{sha\,c_3}|g)P(g). && (6.11) \end{aligned}$$

The formulation above allows us to update the probability of each image being a target based on the updated probabilities of the cluster to which it belongs and the relevance of each feature. In our implementation of the algorithm we chose not to update the individual probabilities of each image, but instead to stop at the cluster level. By doing so, we hope to reduce the computational cost and allow a better display update strategy to be used without sacrificing the quality of the results or the effectiveness of the approach.

4.3.1 A Numerical Example

Let us assume a database of size $n = 100$, whose images have been grouped in $K_1 = 4$ clusters according to color, $K_2 = 3$ clusters according to texture, and $K_3 = 5$ clusters according to shape. The size of each cluster $\| C_{gj} \|$, where g is the visual property under which the images were clustered ($g \in \{col, tex, sha\}$) and j is the cluster number under that same property is given below:

Color	*Texture*	*Shape*
$\| C_{col1} \|= 40$	$\| C_{tex1} \|= 50$	$\| C_{sha1} \|= 40$
$\| C_{col2} \|= 30$	$\| C_{tex2} \|= 40$	$\| C_{sha2} \|= 30$
$\| C_{col3} \|= 20$	$\| C_{tex3} \|= 10$	$\| C_{sha3} \|= 20$
$\| C_{col4} \|= 10$		$\| C_{sha4} \|= 6$
		$\| C_{sha5} \|= 4$

In the first iteration, one representative from each color-based cluster is displayed to the user. Let us assume that $N = 4$ and call these images x_1, x_2, x_3, and x_4. Let us assume that the mapping between each of these images and the triple containing the numbers of the clusters to which it belongs is the one shown below:

Image	*triple*
x_1	$\{1,1,1\}$
x_2	$\{2,2,2\}$
x_3	$\{3,1,5\}$
x_4	$\{4,3,1\}$

Moreover, let us assume that the user rated image x_1 as good (i.e., $r_1 = g$), x_4 as bad (i.e., $r_4 = b$), and the other two as indifferent (i.e., $r_2 = r_3 = i$).

The first part of the **UpdateProbabilities()** function will update the probability of each cluster to which the good and bad examples belong according to the following calculations:

Cluster	$P(c_{gj})$ *before*	$P(c_{gj})$ *after*	*Normalized* $P(c_{gj})$ *after*
C_{col1}	0.400	0.800	0.590
C_{col2}	0.300	0.300	0.222
C_{col3}	0.200	0.200	0.151
C_{col4}	0.100	0.050	0.037
C_{tex1}	0.500	1.000	0.690
C_{tex2}	0.400	0.400	0.276
C_{tex3}	0.100	0.050	0.034
C_{sha1}	0.400	0.400	0.400
C_{sha2}	0.300	0.300	0.300
C_{sha3}	0.200	0.200	0.200
C_{sha4}	0.060	0.060	0.060
C_{sha5}	0.040	0.040	0.040

The second part of the **UpdateProbabilities()** function will call **UpdatePf()** and update the probability of each feature being relevant according to the table below:

Feature	*P(g) before*	*P(g) after*	*Normalized P(g) after*
Color	$0.\bar{3}$	$0.\bar{6}$	$0.\bar{4}$
Texture	$0.\bar{3}$	$0.\bar{6}$	$0.\bar{4}$
Shape	$0.\bar{3}$	$0.1\bar{6}$	$0.\bar{1}$

Then, the product $P(C_{gj}|g)P(g)$ will be updated for all clusters, and the partial results will be the ones indicated below:

Cluster	$P(C_{gj}|g)P(g)$
C_{col1}	0.262
C_{col2}	0.099
C_{col3}	0.067
C_{col4}	0.016
C_{tex1}	0.306
C_{tex2}	0.123
C_{tex3}	0.015
C_{sha1}	0.044
C_{sha2}	0.033
C_{sha3}	0.022
C_{sha4}	0.006
C_{sha5}	0.004

All the clusters are then sorted according to their current value of $P(C_{gj}|g)P(g)$ (below) and the **DisplayNextBestImages()** function chooses the next images to be displayed. The first two images would come from cluster C_{tex1}, the third from cluster C_{col1}, and the fourth from cluster C_{tex2}.

Cluster	$P(C_{gj}|g)P(g)$
C_{tex1}	0.306
C_{col1}	0.262
C_{tex2}	0.123
C_{col2}	0.099
C_{col3}	0.067
C_{sha1}	0.044
C_{sha2}	0.033
C_{sha3}	0.022
C_{col4}	0.016
C_{tex3}	0.015
C_{sha4}	0.006
C_{sha5}	0.004

Let us now assume two not yet displayed images T_p and T_q, where $1 \leq p, q \leq n$, $p \neq q$, whose triples containing the numbers of the clusters to which each of them belongs are shown below:

Image	triple
T_p	$\{1, 2, 3\}$
T_q	$\{4, 2, 1\}$

Let us analyze their cluster memberships in more detail:

T_p belongs to the same color cluster of an image labeled as ***good*** by the user in the previous iteration, to the same texture cluster as an image labeled indifferent, and to a shape cluster from which no representative has yet been seen by the user.

T_q, on the other hand, belongs to the same color cluster of an image labeled as ***bad*** by the user in the previous iteration, to the same texture cluster as an image labeled indifferent, and to a shape cluster from which two representatives have previously been seen by the user, one of which was labeled *good*, the other *bad*.

It is intuitively expected that, based on the information learned by the system so far, T_p is more likely to be the target than T_q.

If we follow the mathematical formulation of our algorithm all the way to the image level, we get:

$$\begin{aligned} P(T_p = T) &= P(T_p|C_{colc_1})P(C_{colc_1}|g)P(g) + \\ &\quad P(T_p|C_{texc_2})P(C_{texc_2}|g)P(g) + \\ &\quad P(T_p|C_{shac_3})P(C_{shac_3}|g)P(g) \\ &= (1/40 * 0.59 * 0.\bar{4}) + \\ &\quad (1/40 * 0.276 * 0.\bar{4}) + \\ &\quad (1/20 * 0.2 * 0.\bar{1}) \\ &= 0.0107\bar{3}, \end{aligned}$$

which is greater than the a priori probability assigned to each image in the database, 0.01, as expected.

$$\begin{aligned} P(T_q = T) &= P(T_q|C_{colc_1})P(C_{colc_1}|g)P(g) + \\ &\quad P(T_q|C_{texc_2})P(C_{texc_2}|g)P(g) + \\ &\quad P(T_q|C_{shac_3})P(C_{shac_3}|g)P(g) \\ &= (1/10 * 0.037 * 0.\bar{4}) + \\ &\quad (1/40 * 0.276 * 0.\bar{4}) + \\ &\quad (1/40 * 0.4 * 0.\bar{1}) \\ &= 0.0058\bar{2}, \end{aligned}$$

which is less than the a priori probability assigned to each image in the database, 0.01, as expected.

If we trace the pseudocode for the abbreviated version of the algorithm, stopping at the cluster level, and picking the next best representatives, we will conclude that T_p has two chances of being picked for display at the next iteration, either as the third image (because it belongs to C_{col1}) or as the fourth (because it also belongs to C_{tex2}), while T_p has only one chance of being chosen, as the fourth image (because it also belongs to C_{tex2}).

This conclusion does not mean, however, that T_p is twice more likely to be chosen for display during the following iteration than T_q, because the samples from each cluster are not chosen at random, but rather based on their dissimilarity to that cluster's medoid. In other words, if T_p does not qualify as the "not previously displayed image from cluster C_{col1} with lowest dissimilarity from its medoid" and T_q is closer to the medoid of cluster C_{tex2} than T_p, it is certain that T_p will not be displayed while it is possible that T_q will be chosen as the fourth image.

In either case, the system would correctly rank T_p better than T_q, but using the latest display update strategy, the mapping between the image's current ranking and the selection of next images to be displayed would not be as direct as in the RF mode.

4.4 Display Update Strategy

The original display update algorithm displays the best partial results based on a ranked list of images, sorted by the probability of being the target. It is a straightforward approach, but it has its disadvantages. It is inherently greedy, which may leave the user in a very uncomfortable position.

Suppose, for example, that the user is searching for the Canadian flag in a database that has only one instance of the desired flag and tens of images of a baby in red clothes. Assume that the first random subset of images contains one of such baby images (Figure 6.17). In an attempt to help the system converge to the Canadian flag, the user labels the baby picture as good (based on the amount of red it contains). The display update algorithm will show many other images of the baby in red clothes during the next iteration (Figure 6.18), which leaves the user with restricted options: if she labels those images as *good* — as she did before — the system will bring more and more of those; if she labels them as *bad*, the system might assume that the red component is not as important, which would likely move the Canadian flag image down the list of best candidates.

To overcome this limitation, we designed an alternative display update strategy, that relies on clustering and displays the next set of images according to the algorithm presented in Figure 6.19. This algorithm explicitly prevents too many images that look alike to be displayed simultaneously on the browser's side. Its main advantage is that it gives the user a larger variety of images to choose from at each iteration. The

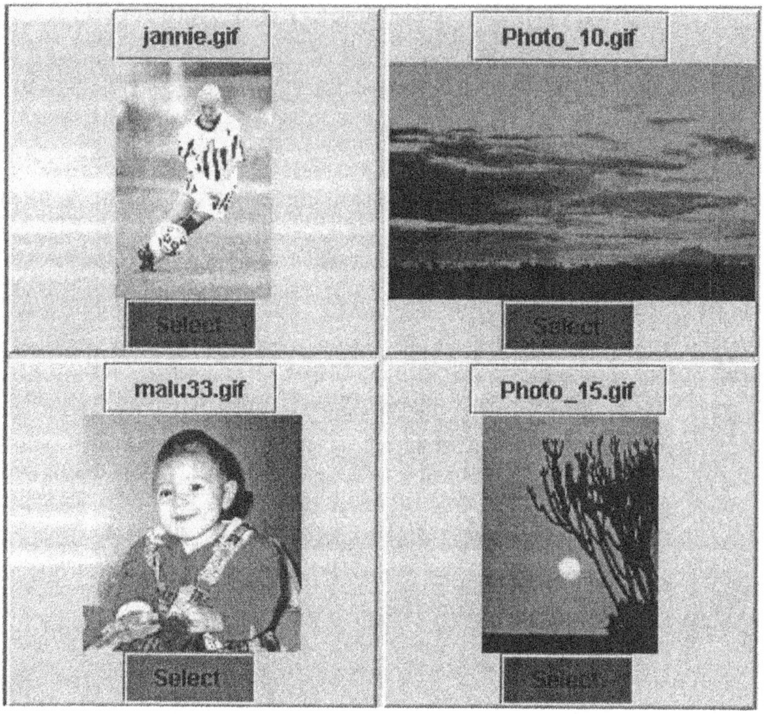

Figure 6.17. Limitations of the original display update algorithm. The user — searching for the Canadian flag — selects the lower-left image as *good* based on the amount of red it contains.

drawback is that the user might lose the feeling that the system is actually learning anything and converging to the desired target, which is apparent in the display strategy used in the RF mode.

5. Experiments and Results

This section presents selected results of some of the experiments to which MUSE has been submitted, and conclusions that can be derived from them. It has been divided into five subsections. It starts with the results of experiments in RF mode. Next, a summary of the tests in QBE mode is presented. Those tests' goal was to evaluate the quality of features, distance measurements, and their combinations. It then presents tests on the candidate clustering algorithm, PAM, performed before we officially decided to use it in our RFC mode. Subsection 5.4 reports the results of experiments in RFC mode. After having tested the RF and RFC modes individually, we decided to combine ideas from the two and test it. Tests on this "mixed mode" are reported in Subsection 5.5.

Figure 6.18. Limitations of the original display update algorithm (*continued*). The display update algorithm fills the whole browser area with images that are very much alike, but do not correspond to the user's desired target.

Along these tests we used one or more of the following databases:

Database name	*Size (number of images)*
PAM	10
DEBUG[14]	32
HUNDRED	100
SMALL	116
MTAP	1,100
MUSE11K	11,129

[14]This small database was especially crafted to test the clustering algorithm from a human perception point of view and for debugging purposes.

```
DisplayNextBestImages() {
    Sort all clusters in descending order
    according to P(cg)*P(g);

    Fill the first half of the screen with (not previously
    displayed) images from the top-most cluster, starting
    from the one with lowest dissimilarity from its medoid.

    Fill the third quarter of the screen with (not
    previously displayed) images from the second-best
    cluster, starting from the one with lowest
    dissimilarity from its medoid.

    Fill the remaining screen positions with not
    previously displayed images from each remaining cluster.
}
```

Figure 6.19. Pseudocode for the **DisplayNextBestImages()** function.

5.1 Testing the System in RF Mode

We performed several tests on the first proposed model of relevance feedback under the "target testing" paradigm [43], in which the CBVIR system's effectiveness is measured as the average number of images that a user must examine in searching for a given random target. For each experiment, the number of iterations required to locate the target is compared against the baseline case (a purely random search for the target) for the same conditions.

Our fundamental figure of merit is *effectiveness* (ε), defined as:

$$\varepsilon = \frac{N_r}{N_f} \tag{6.12}$$

where: N_r is the average number of iterations required to find the target in random mode and N_f is the average number of iterations required to find the target in relevance feedback mode. Larger values of ε mean better performance.

The different tests attempted to provide insightful answers to important questions such as:

- Does the system always outperform the baseline case? By how much?
- What is the influence of the target image on the system's performance?

a. Canada

b. Sunset05

Figure 6.20. Sample target images.

- How well does the system scale when the database grows in size?
- Is there an optimal value of number of images to be displayed to the user in each iteration? If so, what is it?
- What is the relationship between the feature vectors used to characterize images' contents and the performance of the system?
- From a user's point of view, how do the user's style relate to the performance of the system?

5.1.1 Preliminary Tests

At its very early stage MUSE was tested using the *SMALL* database, the HSV+ feature vector (consisting of normalized pixel count in each of the 12 partitions of the HSV space plus global brightness and saturation information), and nine images per iteration. Table 6.2 summarizes the results for two different target images (Canada, Figure 6.20(a), and Sunset05, Figure 6.20(b)). For each set of 20 trials, it shows the best, worst, and average results (expressed in terms of number of iterations, where each iteration shows nine new images to the user) and the corresponding effectiveness. For a random search with nine images per iteration and a database of 116 images, the theoretical average number of iterations required to find the target in random mode (N_r) is 6.444.

These results reveal an apparent dependency between the target image and the system's effectiveness. Our results[15] suggest that it is easier to find the target when:

[15]The results referred to here include tests with other target images not reported in this book.

Table 6.2. Target testing results after 20 trials per target image, for a database of 116 images, using partitioning of HSV space, and nine images per iteration.

Target image	*Best result*	*Worst result*	*Average* (N_f)	*Effectiveness* (ε)
Canada	2	3	2.20	2.929
Sunset05	1	7	3.60	1.790

- The target image belongs to a reasonably large semantic category, from which there are good and bad examples.
- The target image has few, well-defined, properties (few relevant colors, few objects, etc.)
- A vast majority of the image's pixels map the object(s) of interest in the scene, in other words the object(s) of interest appear(s) larger than the background.
- The actual color properties of the image match our belief of what they are. For example, when looking for the image in Figure 6.21(a) we might fail to realize that the grass is not exactly green. Our bias in thinking so might make it harder for us to understand that images such as the one in Figure 6.21(b) are not exactly good examples, if we are looking for the image in Figure 6.21(a).

Nevertheless, the system outperformed a purely random search by a factor of 2.222 (in average), and in only one of the 40 trials the total number of iterations was greater than the baseline case, which is encouraging.

5.1.2 Increasing Database Size

After having proven the basic concept using a small database, we decided to test MUSE with a larger database, which we called MTAP — a repository of 1,100 images, most of which belonged to 11 completely disparate semantic categories with approximately 100 images per category. All the other parameters (HSV+ feature vector, nine images per iteration, target images) remained the same.

Table 6.3 summarizes the results of these tests. For a random search with nine images per iteration and a database of 1,100 images, the theoretical average number of iterations required to find the target in random mode (N_r) is 61.111.

The impact of the increase in database size on the overall effectiveness was better than we expected. The system outperformed a purely random

Figure 6.21. The grass is not always green... The image on the right is not as good an example when searching for the image on the left as we might think.

Table 6.3. Target testing results after 20 trials per target image, for a database of 1100 images, using partitioning of HSV space, and nine images per iteration.

Target image	*Best result*	*Worst result*	*Average* (N_f)	*Effectiveness* (ε)
Canada	2	28	12.35	4.948
Sunset05	5	46	24.00	2.546

search by a factor of 3.362 (in average), and in none of the 40 trials the total number of iterations was greater than the baseline case. These results also confirm the previous findings related to the dependency on the target image (results for the Canadian flag are still better than the ones obtained with the sunset image).

5.1.3 Improving the Color-Based Feature Set

The HSV+ feature vector is limited in its ability to classify images according to the human perception of their color contents, which led us to replace the original color-based 14-element feature vector by a 64-bin RGB color histogram. We ran a new set of tests on the system in RF mode using the new feature vector over the *MTAP* image database. All

Table 6.4. Target testing results after 20 trials per target image, for a database of 1100 images, using color histogram, and nine images per iteration.

Target image	*Best result*	*Worst result*	*Average* (N_f)	*Effectiveness* (ε)
Canada	1	18	7.70	7.937
Sunset05	1	16	6.70	9.121

the other parameters (nine images per iteration, target images) remained the same. The results are summarized in Table 6.4. Overall, they were significantly better than the ones reported in Table 6.3, confirming our expectation of better performance thanks exclusively to better quality features.

5.1.4 Evaluating the Influence of the Number of Images per Iteration

MUSE has an option that allows the user to set the number of images displayed on the browser's side. The current options are: four, nine or 25. In RF mode it translates into the number of images displayed back to user at each iteration. We were interested in evaluating the impact of this choice on the system's effectiveness. There is an obvious trade-off between the number of images per iteration and the expected number of iterations until the user finds the target. What is not so obvious, however, is how the users react when they have the option of answering more questions per iteration aiming at reaching the target in less time. We ran another set of tests on the system in RF mode using the same target images, color histogram as the feature vector, and the *MTAP* image database.

The results are summarized in Table 6.5. Even though we expected them to be comparable to the ones reported in Table 6.4, they turned out being better by a factor between 18% and 25%, which was somehow surprising. Our current explanation for this improved performance is that certain human factors — fatigue, possibility of being confused by too many images, difficulty to keep consistency in *good* and *bad* ratings, among others — that are more likely to occur when processing more images per iteration might have been responsible for this improved performance for the case with less images per iteration. There are many open questions here that might be subject of future research by psychologists and researchers of human-machine interaction.

Table 6.5. Target testing results after 20 trials per target image, for a database of 1100 images, using color histogram, and four images per iteration.

Target image	*Best result*	*Worst result*	*Average* (N_f)	*Effectiveness* (ε)
Canada	2	43	14.60	9.418
Sunset05	4	27	12.05	11.411

5.1.5 Testing the Relationship Between the User's Style and System Performance

Since MUSE allows and expects its users to express their understanding of good and bad examples, and considering the fact that different users will behave differently when requested to indicate their preferences, we decided to run another set of tests to simulate different users with different attitudes towards the system:

- *cautious* (a user who selects very few good and bad examples),
- *moderate* (a user who picks few examples of each),
- *aggressive* (a user who chooses as many good and bad examples as appropriate), and
- *semantic* (a user who would consider an image to be a good example if it had similar semantic meaning *and* color composition, would do nothing for an image whose only similarities are color-related *or* semantic, and would tag as *bad* any image that has nothing in common with the target).

Using only one target image (Canada), the *HUNDRED* database, the HSV+ feature vector, four images per iteration, and fewer trials per profile (10), we simulated each profile and obtained the results shown in Table 6.6. They are comparable to the ones reported in Table 6.2 and suggest that the system performs best for the *aggressive* case, which can be interpreted as "the more information a user provides per iteration, the faster the system will converge", which is intuitively fine. The performance for the *semantic* case ranks as second best, which is also encouraging. In this case, the value of N_r is 12.5 iterations.

5.1.6 A Note About Convergence

In order to inspect how MUSE converges towards the desired target, we implemented a debugging option that allows us to check the current

Table 6.6. Target testing results for different user profiles, using a 100 image database, 10 trials per profile, four images per iteration, and searching for the Canadian flag.

Profile	*Best result*	*Worst result*	*Average* (N_f)	*Effectiveness* (ε)
Cautious	2	9	4.90	2.551
Moderate	2	7	4.20	2.976
Aggressive	1	6	3.40	3.676
Semantic	3	6	3.90	3.205

ranking of the target image at the end of each iteration. Figure 6.22 shows the results of two different trials within the same context (color histogram as a feature vector, 1,100 image database, the Canadian flag as a target image, nine images per iteration, and seven iterations to reach the target).

Case A shows the desired behavior: the ranking of the target image improves monotonically after each user's action. Case B shows an example of oscillatory behavior towards the target. Table 6.7 shows the results, expressed in percentage form, for 120 independent trials, using different target images, number of images per iteration (N), and feature vectors (FV), HSV+ or color histogram (Hist). After 120 trials against the same 1,100 image database, most of them (62.5%) behaved as in case B, which gives an indication of the convergence properties of MUSE. We believe that the main reasons for this oscillatory behavior can be: imperfect match between the user's perception of an image and the system's understanding of that image's features (the values are better for histogram-based tests than for HSV-based ones), the amount of information learned by the system at each iteration (the results are better for nine images per iteration when using histogram-based features), and human factors (fatigue, inconsistency, and others). Some of these factors and their impact in the design of CBVIR systems might undergo further research in the future.

5.2 Testing Features and Distance Measurements

We carried out extensive tests on the quality of the feature extraction and distance measurement algorithms and their suitability to the CBVIR problem. Using MUSE's Query-By-Example (QBE) mode, we tested 50 different combinations of features and distance measures, each of which was tested with 20 different query images. The results are reported and discussed in this section.

Table 6.7. Convergence tests.

Target image	*N*	*FV*	*Case A %*	*Case B %*
Canada	9	HSV+	25	75
Sunset05	9	HSV+	15	85
Canada	9	Hist	50	50
Sunset05	9	Hist	60	40
Canada	4	Hist	25	75
Sunset05	4	Hist	50	50

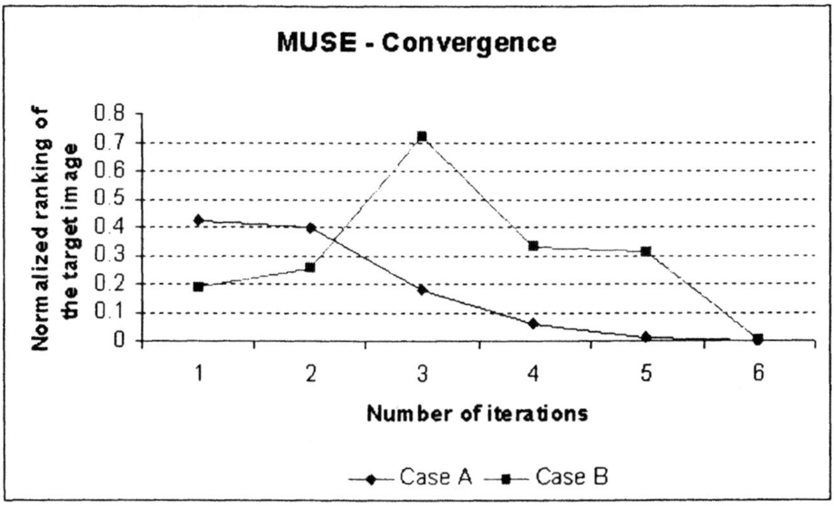

Figure 6.22. Different ways to converge to the target.

5.2.1 Goals and Methodology

1 The Image Database

We used a database of 11,129 images (*MUSE11K*) that includes 11,000 images from Corel Gallery — divided into 110 semantic categories as diverse as "Alaskan wildlife" or "Marble textures" — and 129 other images, including synthetic images created for the sake of debugging some of our algorithms. It is a very heterogeneous database, which should account for a fair evaluation of the various feature extraction and dissimilarity calculation methods.

2 The Benchmark

We developed a benchmark consisting of 20 queries, each with a unique correct answer identified by hand from *MUSE11K* before running any experiments. The queries were chosen to represent various situations such as different views of the same scene, changes in appearance, brightness, and sharpness, zoom in and zoom out, cropping, rotation, among many others. These data serve as ground truth to test different image feature and distance measurement combinations.

3 Features

We used the following feature extraction methods, alone or combined:

- Partitioning of the HSV space (**HSV+**).
- Color histogram (**Hist**), using the RGB color model and 64 bins.
- Color histogram with a simple color constancy algorithm described in [166] (**HistCC**).
- A 64-bin color autocorrelogram (**Correl**) for 4 different distance values ($D = \{1, 3, 5, 7\}$).
- A 20-element texture descriptor (**Text**) that uses the variance of the gray level co-occurrence matrix for five distances (d) and four different orientations (θ) as a measure of the texture properties of an image.
- A simple edge/shape descriptor (**Shape**), consisting of a normalized count of the number of edge pixels obtained by applying the Sobel edge-detection operators in eight different directions (0°, 45°, 90°, 135°, 180°, 225°, 270°, and 315°) and thresholding the results.

4 Distance Measures

The distance measures between two n-dimensional feature vectors, $\mathbf{x}_1$ and $\mathbf{x}_2$ were:

- Manhattan distance, also known as the L_1 norm:

$$d_M(\mathbf{x}_1, \mathbf{x}_2) = \sum_{i=1}^{i=n} |\mathbf{x}_1[i] - \mathbf{x}_2[i]| \qquad (6.13)$$

- Euclidean distance, also known as the L_2 norm:

$$d_E(\mathbf{x}_1, \mathbf{x}_2) = \sqrt{\sum_{i=1}^{i=n} (\mathbf{x}_1[i] - \mathbf{x}_2[i])^2} \qquad (6.14)$$

- Histogram intersection, originally proposed by Swain and Ballard [166]:

$$H(\mathbf{x}_1, \mathbf{x}_2) = \frac{\sum_{i=1}^{i=n} \min(\mathbf{x}_1[i], \mathbf{x}_2[i])}{\sum_{i=1}^{i=n} \mathbf{x}_1[i]} \tag{6.15}$$

- d_1 distance, first proposed by Huang[85], and defined as:

$$d_1(\mathbf{x}_1, \mathbf{x}_2) = \sum_{i=1}^{i=n} \frac{|\mathbf{x}_1[i] - \mathbf{x}_2[i]|}{1 + \mathbf{x}_1[i] + \mathbf{x}_2[i]} \tag{6.16}$$

5 Performance Measures

The image retrieval problem under the QBE paradigm can be described as: let $\mathcal{D}$ be an image database and $\mathcal{Q}$ be the query image. Obtain a permutation of the images in $\mathcal{D}$ based on $\mathcal{Q}$, i.e., assign $rank(\mathcal{I}) \in [|\mathcal{D}|]$ for each $\mathcal{I} \in \mathcal{D}$, using some notion of similarity to $\mathcal{Q}$. This problem is usually solved by sorting the images $\mathcal{I} \in \mathcal{D}$ according to $|f(\mathcal{I}) - f(\mathcal{Q})|$, where $f(\cdot)$ is a function computing feature vectors of images and $|\cdot|_f$ is some distance metric defined on feature vectors.

Let $\{\mathcal{Q}_1, \ldots, \mathcal{Q}_q\}$ be the set of query images. For a query $\mathcal{Q}_i$, let $\mathcal{I}_i$ be the unique correct answer. We use two measures to evaluate the overall performance of a feature vector–distance metric combination:

(a) *r-measure* of a method which sums up over all queries, the rank of the correct answer, i.e.,

$$r = \sum_{i=1}^{q} rank(\mathcal{I}_i) \tag{6.17}$$

We also use the average r-measure, $\bar{r}$ which is the r-measure divided by the number of queries q:

$$\bar{r} = r/q \tag{6.18}$$

(b) *p_1-measure* of a method which is the sum (over all queries) of the precision at recall equal to 1:

$$p_1 = \sum_{i=1}^{q} 1/rank(\mathcal{I}_i) \tag{6.19}$$

The average p_1-measure is the p_1-measure divided by q:

$$\bar{p_1} = p_1/q \tag{6.20}$$

Table 6.8. Performance of various color-based methods using Euclidean distance.

Method	**HSV+**	**Hist**	**HistCC**	**Correl**
avg r-measure	379.1	317.0	**147.9**	268.7
avg p_1-measure	0.193	**0.446**	0.229	0.375

Images ranked at the top contribute more to the p_1-measure. A method is good if it has a low r-measure and a high p_1-measure. From a VIR point of view, a low r-measure means that in average the desired image will be ranked among the best while a high p_1-measure can be interpreted as "either the desired image is found and ranked among the very top or it is missed by many positions". Since there is no guarantee that a particular feature–distance combination will be best from both perspectives, the question is: which one should we give preference to? Our answer to this question is: if the user is interested in a particular image (target search paradigm), we should give preference to the method that maximizes the average p_1-measure; if the user is looking for images that resemble the one she has in mind (similarity search paradigm), she might prefer the combination that minimizes the average r-measure, based on the fact that the desired image will be — in average — well ranked, and the ones ranked above it might bear enough similarity to be picked instead of the originally desired target.

5.2.2 Color-Based Methods

Table 6.8 summarizes the results for average r-measure and average p_1-measure of experiments designed to test the quality of different candidates for color-based feature extraction methods. The algorithms tested here are: **HSV+**, **Hist**, **HistCC**, and **Correl**. The distance metric used is Euclidean.

The color histogram method performed best according to the p_1-measure while its variant with color constancy algorithm performed best according to the r-measure. Color correlogram ranked second from both standpoints, while partitioning of HSV showed the worst results. Based on these results, the HSV+ method was discarded and not tested any further.

Table 6.9. Performance of texture- and shape-based methods using Euclidean distance.

Method	**Text**	**Shape**	**Text + Shape**
avg r-measure	2133.6	**1254.9**	2133.6
avg p_1-measure	**0.112**	0.016	**0.112**

Table 6.10. Performance of **Hist** plus shape and/or texture combinations using Euclidean distance.

Method	**Hist**	**Hist+Text**	**Hist+Shape**	**Hist+Text+Shape**
avg r-measure	317.0	2641.2	**160.9**	2641.1
avg p_1-measure	0.446	0.112	**0.469**	0.112

5.2.3 Shape or Texture Only

Before attempting to combine color information with shape and/or texture, we decided to test our texture-based and shape-based candidate features separately to investigate the quality of the results they produce. These results are reported in Table 6.9.

The results show that shape alone performs best from a r-measure point of view while texture — either alone or combined with shape — performs best according to the p_1-measure. Moreover, adding them together moved the overall performance down, which is primarily a problem related to the distance metric used. The same combination with a better metric — d_1 distance — (see section 5.2.5) produces intermediate results, as one would intuitively expect.

5.2.4 Combining Color, Texture, and Shape

It is expected that adding shape and/or texture detection capabilities to a color-based CBVIR system should improve the quality of its results. This section reports tests on combinations of color-based methods alone and combined with shape and/or texture information. The distance used is Euclidean.

Table 6.10 shows the results of adding shape and/or texture to color histogram. Table 6.11 reports the results of adding shape and/or texture to color histogram with color constancy algorithm. Finally, Table 6.12 shows the results of adding shape and/or texture to color correlogram.

Table 6.11. Performance of **HistCC** (**HCC**) plus shape (**S**) and/or texture (**T**) combinations using Euclidean distance.

Method	HCC	HCC + T	HCC + S	HCC + T + S
avg r-measure	147.9	2641.0	**65.8**	2641.0
avg p_1-measure	0.229	0.112	**0.254**	0.112

Table 6.12. Performance of **Correl** plus shape (**S**) and/or texture (**T**) combinations using Euclidean distance.

Method	Correl	Correl+T	Correl+S	Correl+T+S
avg r-measure	268.7	2639.5	**216.4**	2639.4
avg p_1-measure	0.375	0.112	**0.399**	0.112

Analysis of the results from Tables 6.10, 6.11, and 6.12 shows that the combination of any color-based feature with the shape descriptor helped improve both the r-measure and p_1-measure figures. The combination **HistCC + Shape** is the best overall in terms of r-measure while the combination **Hist + Shape** has the highest values of p_1-measure.

5.2.5 Distance Measures

The tests reported in Table 6.13 compare the performance of each feature combination according to three different metrics: Euclidean, Manhattan, and d_1.

These results show that:

- The best overall combination according to the r-measure is **HistCC + Shape** with Euclidean distance measurements and the the best overall combination according to the p_1-measure is **Hist + Shape** with d_1 distance measurements.

- For almost all the combinations involving texture, the use of d_1 distance improved both the r-measure as well as the p_1-measure. The only exception was the decrease in the p_1-measure when texture is used alone.

The two pairs that ranked best in terms of average rank were the ones shown in Figure 6.23(a) and (b), respectively. While the second pair might look like an "easy" one (high contrast between foreground

Table 6.13. Performance of different distance measurements.

Features	*Euclidean*		*Manhattan*		d_1	
	avg r	avg p_1	avg r	avg p_1	avg r	avg p_1
HSV+	379.1	0.193	371.6	0.187	331.4	0.183
Hist	317.0	0.446	244.0	0.573	287.8	0.608
HistCC	147.9	0.229	87.8	0.256	70.8	0.260
Correl	268.7	0.375	319.6	0.425	455.0	0.491
Text	2133.6	0.112	2199.1	0.115	1816.8	0.105
Shape	1254.9	0.016	1266.7	0.011	1237.8	0.011
Shape+Text	2133.6	0.112	2197.1	0.115	1740.2	0.132
Hist+Shape	160.9	0.469	90.5	0.580	99.0	**0.617**
Hist+Text	2641.2	0.112	2694.6	0.118	1910.2	0.182
Hist+Shape+Text	2641.1	0.112	2692.3	0.118	1851.2	0.197
HistCC+Shape	**65.8**	0.254	71.9	0.263	90.2	0.283
HistCC+Text	2641.0	0.112	2695.7	0.118	2000.2	0.128
HistCC+Shape+Text	2641.0	0.112	2693.9	0.118	1939.2	0.140
Correl+Shape	216.4	0.399	179.4	0.482	251.3	0.543
Correl+Text	2639.5	0.112	2658.1	0.132	1238.6	0.364
Correl+Shape+Text	2639.4	0.112	2656.0	0.133	1167.9	0.366

and background, stable background, no big changes in size or shape of the main object in the scene), the first pair is not as trivial (there are changes in angle, positions of the main objects, and even aspect ratio between the two scenes) and having ranked best turned out to be a pleasant surprise.

The two pairs in Figure 6.24(a) and (b) were the ones that showed poorest performance. Here again, the results are not as obvious as they might appear at first. The worst pair corresponds to a zoomed-in, cropped, brighter version of the query image. The changes in color composition, average brightness levels, shape and texture between the two images are so big that finding the second image giving the first as a query turned out to be the hardest task overall. The second worst case is a bit surprising because of its color contents. However, the amount of blurring in the query image was enough to fool the shape and texture detectors and move the overall results down.

5.3 Testing the Clustering Algorithm

Once we decided to use clustering techniques to group together images that have similar visual properties and were about to choose PAM to be

a. Best pair overall b. Second best pair overall

Figure 6.23. Best image pairs in QBE mode.

our clustering algorithm, we carried out a few tests to see how well the clustering stage of our solution performed.

a. Worst pair overall

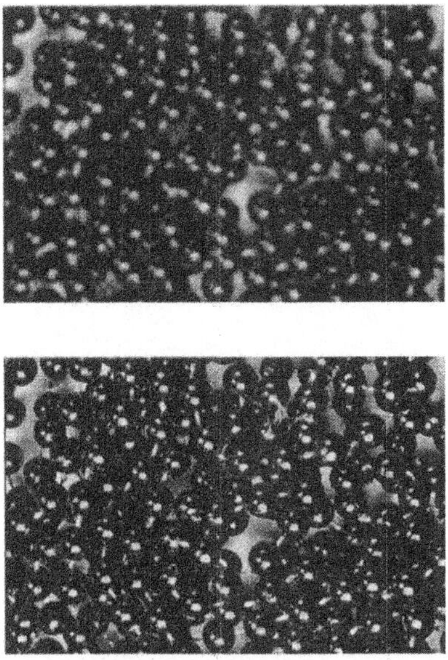

b. Second worst pair overall

Figure 6.24. Image pairs with poorest performance in QBE mode.

We also wanted to test the discriminating power of the *silhouette coefficient* parameter in determining the best value of K (total number of clusters).

Using the PAM database, we tested the PAM algorithm under different combinations of color-based features and distance measures[16].

Tables 6.14, 6.15, 6.16, and 6.17 show the values of the silhouette coefficient for different values of K, from 2 until 9, and different combinations of color-based features and distances.

The results show that different combinations of feature vector and distance measurements give different best values of K. From a qualitative point of view, all the clustering arrangements are fine, but we personally think that the best results were obtained using the HSV+ feature vector, which is rather surprising, considering that its performance in QBE mode was rather poor.

Some conclusions may be derived from these experiments:

- The optimal value of K using silhouette coefficient as a figure of merit indicates the best clustering structure from a purely numerical point

[16]In this case, the distance measures refer to the method used to measure distance between n-dimensional points inside the clustering algorithm as opposed to calculating distances between the feature vectors of two images, as before.

Table 6.14. Silhouette coefficient (*sc*) values for different values of K using 512-bin color histogram and Euclidean distances (Case 1).

K	sc
2	0.35
3	**0.41**
4	0.39
5	0.35
6	0.33
7	0.23
8	0.16
9	0.04

Table 6.15. Silhouette coefficient (*sc*) values for different values of K using the HSV+ feature vector and Euclidean distances (Case 2).

K	sc
2	0.31
3	0.40
4	0.47
5	**0.53**
6	0.42
7	0.40
8	0.31
9	0.16

Table 6.16. Silhouette coefficient (*sc*) values for different values of K using 64-bin color histogram and Euclidean distances (Case 3).

K	sc
2	0.39
3	**0.56**
4	0.43
5	0.47
6	0.38
7	0.33
8	0.25
9	0.17

Table 6.17. Silhouette coefficient (*sc*) values for different values of K using 64-bin color histogram and Manhattan distances (Case 4).

K	sc
2	0.40
3	0.36
4	**0.46**
5	0.40
6	0.34
7	0.32
8	0.24
9	0.17

of view. There is no guarantee that the resulting clusters will be the best from a perceptual viewpoint.

- The same feature vector that showed poor results in QBE mode ended up producing — for this very small database — the best clustering structure from a qualitative point of view.

- Conventional clustering algorithms benefit from more compact feature vectors (result for case 3 is better than cases 1 and 4) and the corresponding reduction in the dimensions of the clustering space. We have a trade-off here: while for QBE purposes we want the richest possible description, for clustering purposes we would settle for the most concise feature vector that still contains enough expressive power about the image contents encoded into it.

We later tested the clustering stage of the new prototype on the *DEBUG* database.

The features used were: 64-bin color histogram for color, the contrast-based 20-element feature vector for texture, and the edge-based 8-element feature vector for shape. The distance measurement used was Euclidean.

Tables 6.18, 6.19, and 6.20 show the values of the silhouette coefficient for different values of K, from 2 until 10, for the color-, texture-, and shape-based feature vectors, respectively.

The results for color-based feature vectors were comparable to the ones we would have obtained had we manually divided our database into eight groups of images. The partitioning of texture- and shape-based feature vectors was not as successful, mostly because of the quality of those vectors.

Table 6.18. Silhouette coefficient (sc) values for different values of K for the color-based feature vector.

K	sc
2	0.404
3	0.408
4	0.483
5	0.498
6	0.521
7	0.531
8	**0.543**
9	0.532
10	0.532

Table 6.19. Silhouette coefficient (sc) values for different values of K for the texture-based feature vector.

K	sc
2	**0.741**
3	0.629
4	0.657
5	0.666
6	0.641
7	0.651
8	0.671
9	0.665
10	0.630

5.4 Testing the System in RFC Mode

We performed several tests on MUSE working on *Relevance Feedback with Clustering* (RFC) mode following the same guidelines used while testing the system in RF mode.

5.4.1 Preliminary Tests

MUSE was tested under the RFC mode using the *DEBUG* database, a combination of color histogram, shape, and texture features, and four images per iteration. Table 6.21 summarizes the results for two different target images (Raspberries, Figure 6.25(a), and Jannie, Figure 6.25(b)). For a random search with four images per iteration and a database of

Table 6.20. Silhouette coefficient (sc) values for different values of K for the shape-based feature vector.

K	sc
2	0.718
3	**0.740**
4	0.554
5	0.588
6	0.547
7	0.498
8	0.521
9	0.565
10	0.551

32 images, the theoretical average number of iterations required to find the target in random mode (N_r) is exactly 4.

Contrary to the operation in RF mode, it was neither necessary nor meaningful to run 20 trials for each image. Since we are dealing with a very small database, few images per iteration, and especially because the first subset of images is no longer random, but dependent upon the color-based clusters, the system's performance is much more deterministic than in the RF mode. In other words, if in each trial the user is always exposed to the same images in the first iteration and always responds to them in the same way, he will get the same images at the second iteration and so on, for all trials. For this reason we just documented five trials for the first image and 10 for the second. As a consequence of that, the results for effectiveness were published only for the sake of completeness. Even though $\varepsilon \geq 1$ for both cases, the size of the database and the number of iterations were too small to validate these figures. This situation is illustrated in Figure 6.26.

An interesting consequence of the less random behavior of the system in RFC mode is that the number of iterations needed to reach a particular target tends to decrease over time, as the user spends more time trying best combinations of good and bad examples and checking which of these combinations help achieve the target more quickly. An example of such decrease in number of iterations over time when the same user is searching for the same target image (Jannie) several (10) times is shown in Figure 6.27.

a. Raspberries

b. Jannie

Figure 6.25. Sample target images.

Table 6.21. Target testing results for a database of 32 images, using RFC mode, and four images per iteration.

Target image	*Best result*	*Worst result*	*Average* (N_f)	*Effectiveness* (ε)
Raspberries	3	3	3.00	1.333
Jannie	3	6	4.00	1.000

5.4.2 Tests Using a Small Database

MUSE was later tested in RFC mode using the *SMALL* database, a combination of color histogram, shape, and texture features, and nine images per iteration. Table 6.22 summarizes the results for two different target images (Canada, Figure 6.20(a), and Sunset05, Figure 6.20(b)).

For the reasons previously described, it was neither necessary nor meaningful to run 20 trials for each image. Therefore, we just documented one trial for the first image and 10 for the second. As a consequence of that, the results for effectiveness were published only for the sake of completeness and their interpretation should be subject to the same restrictions outlined in Subsection 5.4.1.

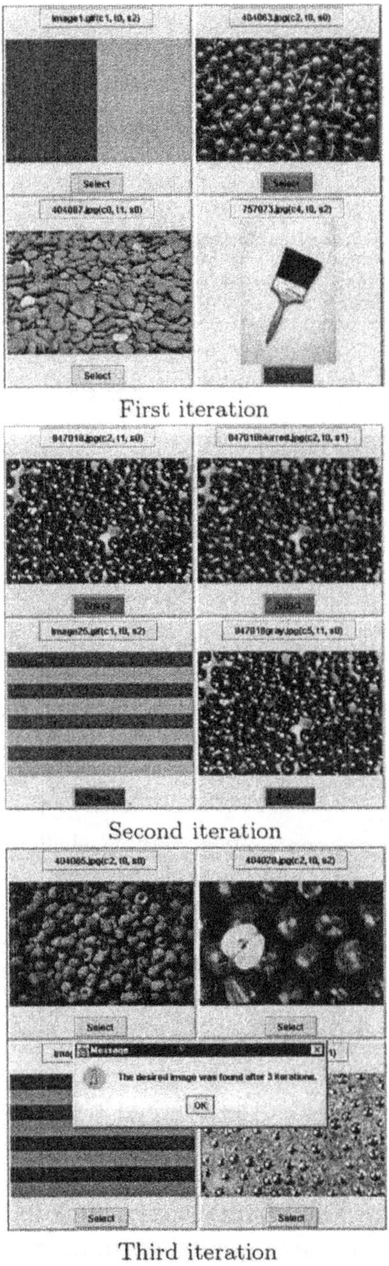

Figure 6.26. Searching for the image with raspberries (found after three iterations).

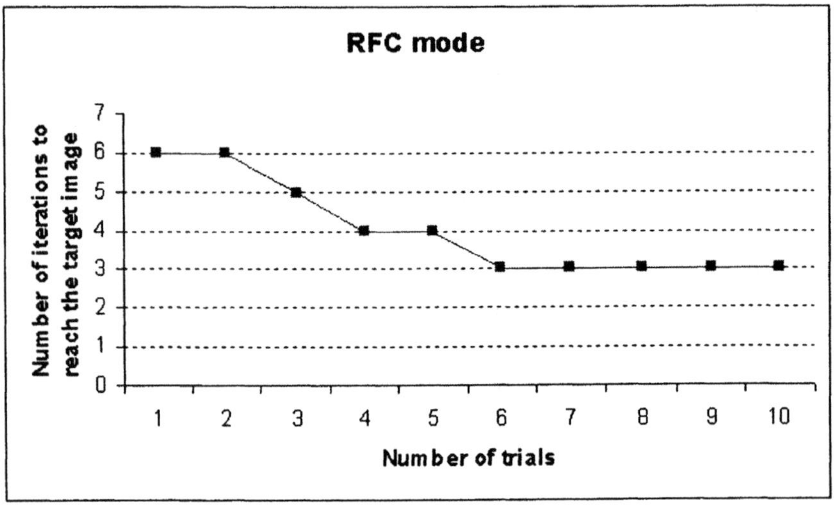

Figure 6.27. Decreasing number of iterations needed to reach the target as the user "learns" how the system works.

Table 6.22. Target testing results for a database of 116 images, using RFC mode, and nine images per iteration.

Target image	*Best result*	*Worst result*	*Average* (N_f)	*Effectiveness* (ε)
Canada	2	2	2.00	3.222
Sunset05	4	5	4.80	1.343

5.4.3 Increasing Database Size

After having proven the basic concept of the new algorithm (RFC mode) using small databases, we decided to test it with the *MTAP* database. All the other parameters remained the same. The first drawback was the realization that the original clustering algorithm (PAM) with its original settings (a range of values for K — between arbitrarily chosen lower and upper limits — from which the best K is chosen based on the silhouette coefficient) would not produce results in a reasonable amount of time. We decided to implement a variant of PAM for large databases, CLARA [91]. CLARA uses a predetermined value of K — $K_1 = K_2 = K_3 = 30$, in this case — and selects a random sample — in our case the sample size is 100 previously extracted feature vectors — from the database. It then runs the (expensive) original

Table 6.23. Target testing results for a database of 1,100 images, using RFC mode, and nine images per iteration.

Target image	*Best result*	*Worst result*	*Average* (N_f)	*Effectiveness* (ε)
Canada	2	28	13.2	4.630
Sunset05	19	75	35.4	1.726

clustering algorithm on those images, grouping them into K_1 clusters according to color, K_2 clusters according to texture, and K_3 clusters according to shape. After the sample images have been clustered, it adds the remaining — 1,000 in this case — images to the existing clustering structure, according to distance calculations between the image and each of the clusters' medoids: the new image is assigned to the cluster whose medoid is closer to the image's feature vector. The process can be repeated for a few independent random samples, and a figure of merit is recorded for each case. The case whose figure of merit is best is used.

Table 6.23 summarizes the results of these tests, with 10 trials for the Canadian flag and five for the sunset image. They confirm the decrease in effectiveness when compared against the results obtained using the RF mode under similar conditions (Table 6.4). The system still outperformed a purely random search by a factor of 2.967 (in average), and in only one of the 15 trials the total number of iterations was greater than the baseline case. Compared to the figures obtained for the tests in RF mode (Table 6.4), however, these results are not as good.

Switching from PAM to CLARA made it necessary to abandon the silhouette coefficient as a figure of merit for choosing the best value of K for a particular data set. We had to arbitrarily choose values for K hoping they would lead to a good distribution of images among groups. Moreover, it introduced a random component — the selection of the 100 samples — with impact on the quality of the clustering. As a consequence of these two factors, the quality of the resulting clusters — which is expected to be the best possible — decreased significantly, hurting the system's performance. Further investigation of clustering algorithms and methods for selecting the ideal value for the number of clusters is under way in order to overcome some of these limitations.

5.5 Mixed Mode Tests

Because of the difficulty in comparing the RFC mode with its deterministic first subset of images against the RF mode with its random

Table 6.24. Target testing results for a database of 1,100 images, using RF mode, a deterministic initial subset of images, and nine images per iteration.

Target image	*Best result*	*Worst result*	*Average* (N_f)	*Effectiveness* (ε)
Canada	3	4	3.4	17.974
Sunset05	3	4	3.2	19.097

selection of images to be displayed first, we decided to add another debugging/testing option to the RF mode that allows it to start with the same images that would be chosen by the system in RFC mode. By doing so, we could test how well does the RF mode behave when it is given the same starting subset of images as the RFC mode. As a consequence of that, we understand that a meaningful comparison between the old and the new set of algorithms can be obtained by comparing the results from Table 6.23 and Table 6.24, rather than by comparing the results from Table 6.23 and Table 6.4. Table 6.24 summarizes the results of these tests, where each target image was searched for in five trials[17]. Figure 6.28 shows the three iterations needed to find the Canadian flag.

The results reported in Table 6.24 are the best overall, which prompts the following conclusions:

- Starting from a subset of images based on the color clustering instead of a purely random sample caused the performance of the original learning algorithm to improve dramatically, despite the imperfections of the clustering structure.

- The results for effectiveness reported in Table 6.24 are not only important from a numerical point of view, but also from a user interaction vantage point: finding the desired target among 1,100 images within three iterations is very exciting, while waiting 20 or more iterations to reach the target — as in some trials in Table 6.23 — can be rather frustrating.

- This mixed mode can be modified to accommodate slightly different arrangements, such as:

[17] Because of the "learning effect" discussed in section 5.4.1, we decided to limit the number of trials to five for each target image. Had we decided to run more trials, the average number of iterations would asymptotically approximate the value 3.0, making our figures look even better.

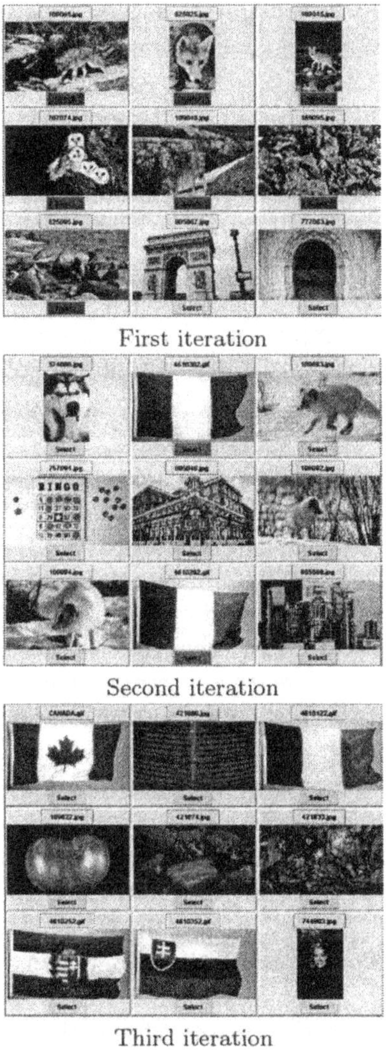

Figure 6.28. Searching for the Canadian flag (found after three iterations).

1 Replacing the automatic clustering algorithm by a manual or semi-automatic clustering of the database (to improve the semantic meaning of each cluster).

2 Using a combination of a (manually or semi-automatically generated) category hierarchy, allowing users to first navigate through the hierarchy until they reach the scope where the content-based search is to be performed.

These and other variations may be subject of future investigation and testing.

6. Summary

This chapter described MUSE, a completely functional CBVIR system with relevance feedback capabilities. Two distinct and completely independent models for solving the image retrieval problem without resorting to metadata and including the user in the loop have been proposed.

1 The first (RF mode) implements an extension of the model originally proposed by Cox et al.[45]. It uses a compact color-based feature vector obtained by partitioning the HSV color space into 12 segments — each of which maps a semantic color — and counting the number of pixels in an image that fall in each segment, plus the global information of average brightness and saturation in the image. It employs a Bayesian learning algorithm which updates the probability of each image in the database being the target based on the user's actions (labeling an image as good, bad, or indifferent). It shows very good results for moderate-size image repositories but does not scale well for larger databases and/or feature vectors. This limitation was one of the motivating factors that led us to the second model (RFC mode).

2 The second (RFC mode) uses a general-purpose clustering algorithm, PAM (Partitioning Around Medoids) [91] — or its variant for large databases, CLARA (Clustering LARge Applications)[91] — and a combination of color-, texture-, and edge(shape)-based features. Each feature vector is extracted independently and applied to the input of the clustering algorithm. This model uses novel (heuristic) approaches to displaying images and updating probabilities that are strongly dependent on the quality of the cluster structure obtained by the clustering algorithm.

Both models assume that the search and retrieval process should be based solely on image contents automatically extracted during the (off-line) feature extraction stage. Moreover, they strive at reducing the burden on the user's side as much as possible, limiting the user's actions to few mouse clicks, and hiding the complexity of the underlying search and retrieval engine from the end user.

Our experiments show that both models exhibit good performance for moderate-size, unconstrained databases. They also provide experimental evidence that a combination of the two outperforms any of them individually, which is encouraging.

Results of experiments with MUSE point to the following conclusions and remarks:

- All variants of MUSE working under the relevance feedback (with or without clustering) paradigm performed better (in average) than a purely random search for the same target images.
- In very few isolated trials the number of iterations needed to reach the target was bigger than the baseline case.
- Scalability is a big issue when developing CBVIR systems. As the database grows in size, there is a corresponding (not necessary linear) increase in computational cost and response time, and decrease in quality of results obtained with a given (combination of) feature(s). These factors combined may cause the performance of a system to worsen, sometimes in an unacceptable way (e.g., when the intermediate results are no longer meaningful to the user or when the response time is intolerably long).
- The relationship between number of images per iteration and overall effectiveness shows that MUSE performs better when the user chooses to see less images per iteration. There is nothing in the algorithm to justify this better behavior, which we believe can be attributed mostly to human factors.
- Testing MUSE in RF (or RFC) mode over many consecutive trials is a tedious and time-consuming process, and several factors at the user's side might possibly influence the system's performance, such as fatigue, boredom, or frustration for not finding the desired image fast enough. As a consequence of this, if we had to embed our knowledge of content-based image retrieval using relevance feedback in a commercial product, we would *not* keep the relevance feedback mode the way it currently is, but instead we would combine it with either QBE and/or navigation by categories and/or other methods that help limiting the scope of the RF-based process to a smaller number of images, and therefore help keeping it simple and short.
- The performance of the chosen clustering algorithm (PAM) for small, well-defined databases was very good from both a qualitative as well as computational point of view. Increasing the database size brought a new range of problems, such as the need to run a less-than-perfect version of PAM for large data sets (CLARA) and the need to arbitrarily determine the values of K (number of clusters). Better and faster clustering schemes are currently being investigated.

- Comparing the performance of the new (RFC) algorithm against the old (RF) and the "mixed mode" variant, we can speculate about possible improvements on the RFC mode to be tested in the future:

  - The current heuristic strategy for updating probabilities might be making too hard (and not necessarily best) decisions, because it is solely based on cluster membership. Since the clustering structure is not perfect, two similar images (to the human eye) might be placed in separate (although close to each other) clusters. A refined version of the algorithm, taking intra- and inter-cluster distances into account shall be investigated.
  - The dissimilarity to the medoid does not mean much, i.e, there is no guarantee that the medoid of a cluster is the best representative of that cluster from a visual perception point of view. Relying on picking images whose distances to the medoid are shorter might be as good as randomly picking another image from the same cluster. Experiments must be performed to test the impact of changing the display update strategy from "picking the not previously displayed image that is closest to the cluster's medoid" to "randomly picking a not previously displayed image from that cluster".

- Some of the main open problems shown by the system in RFC mode are:

  - **The clustering algorithm**. Both PAM and its extension to large databases (CLARA) are partitioning-based methods. They can only find spherical-shaped clusters and are only accurate for small databases and feature vector sizes. A possible improvement in this direction will be the implementation of alternative clustering algorithms that are density-based and/or grid-based. Density-based clustering techniques can find clusters of arbitrary, complex shapes, while grid-based techniques quantize the object space into a finite number of cells that form a grid structure and speed up the processing time.
  - **The choice of K**. Choosing the number of clusters into which a data set is to be partitioned is a classic problem in cluster analysis. We tried to rely on a numerical figure of merit (the silhouette coefficient) to guide the process, but this methodology did not scale well. For larger databases we had to replace PAM by CLARA and make arbitrary choices of K_1, K_2, and K_3, which ended up hurting performance. Now, besides the limitations of the original algorithm for large values of feature vector size, database size,

and K, we also have the randomness of CLARA and the arbitrary choice of K to account for when looking for the possible reasons for the decrease in performance.

- **The quality of the features, particularly texture and shape.** The texture and shape descriptors are not very discriminating (see tests in QBE mode), with the only exception being shape in addition to color histogram. When the resulting texture- and shape-based feature vectors are applied to a clustering algorithm, the problem escalates: we now have a less-than-perfect clustering algorithm working on less-than-perfect feature vectors, so it is not surprising to realize that the results may not be as good as expected. Better shape and texture descriptors are currently being investigated.

- **Users get impatient** when it takes too long to get to the result and the intermediate steps do not indicate that the system is converging towards the desired target. The greedy display update algorithm of the RF mode gives the user the impression of convergence (or not) in a much more intuitive way than the one used in the second model. As a consequence of that, we believe that the display update strategy still needs to be improved upon. We need to strike a balance between the first and second algorithms. Another possible way to cope with this problem would be to switch to direct (image-level) comparison after a given number of iterations or after the number of remaining candidates has been reduced to a certain fraction of the original database size.

7. Future Work

MUSE has laid out the foundation for future work in Visual Information Retrieval within the Department of Computer Science and Engineering at Florida Atlantic University. Many issues related to the general problem of content-based image retrieval are under investigation at the time of this writing. Current and future work on MUSE should proceed in three main directions:

1 **Improvements on current prototype.** The current prototype is being improved in a number of ways, such as:

   - Investigation and implementation of better feature extraction algorithms, particularly for color-spatial dependencies, shape, and texture.

   - Investigation and implementation of better clustering algorithms.

- Investigation and implementation of alternative machine learning strategies, particularly a method to learn the user's preferences and habits along several sessions with the system and improve future performance based on past experience.
- Implementation of object detection, localization, and recognition capabilities.
- Implementation of image processing tools (e.g., crop, blur, change colors) to allow pre-processing of the example image in QBE mode.
- Combination of the QBE and RF modes of operation into a mode that would accept an example image and still allow user feedback as to the quality of the partial results.
- Fine-tuning of the heuristic algorithms for probability and display updating in RF modes.
- Redesign of the existing architecture and extension to a Web-based prototype.
- Extension of the current work to video.

2 **Adaptation / extension to specialized databases and retrieval problems**. The knowledge acquired with the development of MUSE can be extended / adapted to specific retrieval needs, e.g., recognition of crime suspects from a database of mug shots. These specialized versions of MUSE would require investigation of additional features and algorithms as well as fine-tuning of parameters for better performance in the new, more constrained, scenario.

3 **Investigation of human-machine interaction factors**. One of the foreseeable extensions to this work would be an interdisciplinary research project, in which Psychology experts would use MUSE as a product to test user's behavior, measure relevant parameters, and try to infer knowledge about the human visual perception system and the mapping between semantic contents and low-level visual features [128].

Another aspect that could be explored by this future research — especially in RFC mode — is how much the user actually learns how to label examples as good or bad in order to achieve faster results. Our trials in RFC mode indicate that it somehow resembles the learning curve for an electronic game. After several trial-and-error steps, the user learns that labeling images of type A as *good* and images of type B as *bad* will lead to faster results when searching for images of type C. Further investigation on how this takes place inside the user's mind, and how much this knowledge can be used by MUSE, might lead to the implementation of a promising learning scheme with semantic capabilities in future stages of this research.

References

[1] Benchmarking for visual information retrieval. http://www.cs.addressu.edu.hk/~leung/TC-12/benchmark.htm.

[2] Brodatz textures. http://www.ux.his.no/~tranden/brodatz.html.

[3] History of color models. http://www.colorcube.com/articles/models/model.htm.

[4] A. Abdel-Mottaleb, N. Dimitrova, R. Desai, and J. Martino. Conivas: Content-based image and video access system. In *Proc. ACM Multimedia*, pages 427–428, Boston, MA, 1996.

[5] P. Aigrain and P. Joly. The automatic real-time analysis of film editing and transition effects and its applications. *Computer and Graphics*, 18(1):93–103, 1994.

[6] P. Aigrain, P. Joly, and V. Longueville. Medium knowledge-based macro-segmentation of video into sequences. In M. Maybury, editor, *Intelligent Multimedia Information Retrieval*, pages 159–173. 1997.

[7] S. Aksoy and R.M. Haralick. Textural features for image database retrieval. In *Proc. IEEE Workshop on Content-Based Access of Image and Video Libraries*, pages 45–49, 1998.

[8] S. Aksoy and R.M. Haralick. Graph-theoretic clustering for image grouping and retrieval. In *Proceedings of the IEEE Computer Society Conference on Computer Vision and Pattern Recognition*, pages 23–25, Fort Collins, CO, USA, 1999.

[9] A. Akutsu and Y. Tonomura. Video tomography: An efficient method for camerawork extraction and motion analysis. In *Proceedings of the 1st ACM International Multimedia Conference*, pages 349–356, October 1994.

[10] M. Amadasun and R. King. Textural features corresponding to textural properties. *IEEE Transactions on Systems, Man and Cybernetics*, 19(5):1264–1274, October 1989.

[11] E. Ardizzone, M. Cascia, and D. Molinelli. Motion and color based video indexing and retrieval. In *Intl. Conf. on Pattern Recognition*, August 1996.

[12] F. Arman, A. Hsu, and M.-Y. Chiu. Feature management for large video databases. In *Proceedings of the SPIE Conference on Storage and Retrieval for Image and Video Databases I*, pages 2–12, 1993.

[13] J. Bach, C. Fuller, A. Gupta, A. Hampapur, B. Gorowitz, R. Humphrey, R. Jain, and C. Shu. Virage image search engine: an open framework for image management. In *Proceedings of the SPIE, Storage and Retrieval for Image and Video Databases IV, San Jose, CA*, pages 76–87, February 1996.

[14] R. Baeza-Yates and B. Ribeiro-Neto. *Modern Information Retrieval.* Addison-Wesley/ACM Press, New York, 1999.

[15] D. H. Ballard. Generalized Hough transform to detect arbitrary patterns. *IEEE Transactions on Pattern Analysis and Machine Intelligence*, 13(2):111–122, 1981.

[16] N. Beckmann, H.P. Kriegel, R. Schneider, and B. Seeger. The R*-tree: an efficient and robust access method for points and rectangles. In *Proceedings of ACM-SIGMOD International Conference on Management of Data*, pages 322–331, Atlantic address, NJ, 1990.

[17] A. B. Benitez, M. Beigi, and S.-F. Chang. Using relevance feedback in content-based image metasearch. *IEEE Internet Computing*, 2(4):59–69, July/August 1998.

[18] J.L. Bentley. Multidimensional binary search trees used for associative searching. *Communications of the ACM*, 18(9):509–517, September 1975.

[19] A. Berman and L. Shapiro. A flexible image database system for content-based retrieval. *Computer Vision and Image Understanding*, 75(1/2):175–195, 1999.

[20] J.S. Boreczky and L.A. Rowe. Comparison of video shot boundary detection techniques. In *Proceedings of the (SPIE) Conference on Storage and Retrieval for Image and Video Databases*, volume 2670, pages 170–179, February 1996.

[21] J.S. Boreczky and L.D. Wilcox. A Hidden Markov Model framework for video segmentation using audio and image features. In *Proceedings of International Conference on Acoustics, Speech and Signal Processing*, volume 6, pages 3741–3744, 1998.

[22] M. Bouet and C. Djeraba. Visual content based retrieval in an image database with relevant feedback. In *Proceedings of the International Workshop on Multi-Media Database Management Systems*, pages 98–105, 1998.

[23] R. Brunelli and O. Mich. Image retrieval by examples. *IEEE Transactions on Multimedia*, 2(3):164–171, September 2000.

[24] J.M. Buijs and M. Lew. Visual learning of simple semantics in imagescape. In Huijsmans and Smeulders [87], pages 131–138.

[25] C. Carson et al. Blobworld: Image segmentation using expectation-maximization and its application to image querying. `http://www.cs.berkeley.edu/~carson/papers/pami.html`.

[26] C. Carson and V. E. Ogle. Storage and retrieval of feature data for a very large online image collection. *IEEE Computer Society Bulletin of the Technical Committee on Data Engineering*, 19(4):19–27, December 1996.

[27] C. Carson, M. Thomas, S. Belongie, J. M. Hellerstein, and J. Malik. Blobworld: A system for region-based image indexing and retrieval. In Huijsmans and Smeulders [87].

[28] E.Y. Chang, B. Li, and C. Li. Toward perception-based image retrieval. *Proceedings IEEE Workshop on Content-based Access of Image and Video Libraries*, pages 101–105, 2000.

[29] S.-F. Chang. VideoQ: An automated content-based video search system using visual cues. In *Proceedings of the* 5th *ACM International Multimedia Conference*, pages 313–324, New York, November 1997.

[30] S.-F. Chang, A. Eleftheriadis, and R. McClintock. Next-generation content representation, creation and searching for new media applications in education. *Proceedings of the IEEE*, 86(5):884–904, May 1998.

[31] S.-F. Chang, J. R. Smith, M. Beigi, and A. Benitez. Visual information retrieval from large distributed online repositories. *Communications of the ACM*, 40(12):63–71, December 1997.

[32] S.-K Chang, Q.Y. Shi, and C.Y. Yan. Iconic indexing by 2-d strings. *IEEE Transactions on Pattern Analysis and Machine Intelligence*, 9(3):413–428, May 1987.

[33] T. Chang and C.-C. Jay Kuo. Texture analysis and classification with tree-structured wavelet transform. *IEEE Transactions on Image Processing*, 2(4), 1993.

[34] T.-S. Chua, C.-X. Chu, and M. Kankanhalli. Relevance feedback techniques for image retrieval using multiple attributes. In *Proceedings of the International Conference on Multimedia Computing and Systems*, Florence, Italy, 1999.

[35] T.-S. Chua, Kian-Lee Tan, and B.C. Ooi. Fast signature-based color-spatial image retrieval. In *Proceedings in IEEE International Conference on Multimedia Computing and Systems*, pages 362–369, 1997.

[36] G. Ciocca, I. Gagliardi, and R. Schettini. Quicklook: a content-based image retrieval system with learning capabilities. In *Proceedings of the International Conference on Multimedia Computing and Systems*, Florence, Italy, 1999.

[37] G. Ciocca, I. Gagliardi, and R. Schettini. Quicklook2: An integrated multimedia system. *International Journal of Visual Languages and Computing, Special Issue on Multimedia Databases and Image Communication*, in print.

[38] Cobion visual content search. `http://www.cobion.com`.

[39] M. Cooper and J. Foote. Scene boundary detection via video self-similarity analysis. In *Proceedings of International Conference on Image Processing*, volume 3, pages 378–381, 2001.

[40] F.M. Costa. Using color image processing techniques to improve the performance of content-based image retrieval systems. M.Sc. thesis, Florida Atlantic University, 2001.

[41] I. Cox, M. Miller, T. Minka, and P. Yianilos. An optimized interaction strategy for Bayesian relevance feedback. In *Proceedings of the IEEE Computer Society Conference on Computer Vision and Pattern Recognition*, pages 553–558, 1998.

[42] I. J. Cox, M. L. Miller, S. M. Omohundro, and P.N. Yianilos. PicHunter: Bayesian relevance feedback for image retrieval. In *Proceedings of the* 13th *International Conference on Pattern Recognition*, volume 3, pages 361–369, Vienna, Austria, 1996.

[43] I. J. Cox, M. L. Miller, S. M. Omohundro, and P.N. Yianilos. Target testing and the PicHunter Bayesian multimedia retrieval system. In *Advanced Digital Libraries Forum*, Washington D.C., 1996.

[44] I. J. Cox, M. L. Miller, T. Papathomas, J. Ghosn, and P.N. Yianilos. Hidden annotation in content based image retrieval. In *Proceedings of the IEEE Workshop on Content-Based Access of Image and Video Libraries*, pages 76–81, San Juan, Puerto Rico, 1997.

[45] I.J. Cox, M.L. Miller, T.P. Minka, T.V. Papathomas, and P.N. Yianilos. The Bayesian image retrieval system, PicHunter: theory, implementation, and psychophysical experiments. *IEEE Transactions on Image Processing*, 9(1):20–37, January 2000.

[46] S. Dagtas. Models for motion-based video indexing and retrieval. *IEEE Transactions on Image Processing*, 9(1):88–101, January 2000.

[47] A. Dailianas, R. Allen, and P. England. Comparison of automatic video segmentation algorithms. In *Proceedings of SPIE Photonics East*, volume 2615, pages 2–16, Philadelphia, October 1995.

[48] M. Das, E. M. Riseman, and B. Draper. Focus: Searching for multi-colored objects in a diverse image database. In *Proceedings of the IEEE Conference on Computer Vision and Pattern Recognition '97*, pages 756–761, June 1997.

[49] A. Del Bimbo. *Visual Information Retrieval.* Morgan Kaufmann, San Francisco, CA, 1999.

[50] A. Del Bimbo, M. Mugnaini, P. Pala, and F. Turco. Picasso: Visual querying by color perceptive regions. In *Proceedings of the 2nd International Conference on Visual Information Systems, San Diego, December '97*, pages 125–131, 1997.

[51] A. Del Bimbo, E. Vicario, and D. Zingoni. Symbolic description and visual querying of image sequences using spatio-temporal logic. *IEEE Transactions on Knowledge and Data Engineering*, 7(4):609–622, August 1995.

[52] E. Di Sciascio, G. Mingolla, and M. Mongiello. Content-based image retrieval over the web using query by sketch and relevance feedback. In Huijsmans and Smeulders [87], pages 123–130.

[53] N. Dimitrova and F. Golshani. Rx for semantic video database retrieval. In *Proceedings of the 2nd ACM international conference on Multimedia*, pages 219–226, San Francisco, 1994.

[54] J.P. Eakins and M.E. Graham. Content-based image retrieval, a report to the JISC technology application programme. Technical report, Institute for Image Data Research, University of Northumbria at Newcastle, UK, January 1999. `http://www.unn.ac.uk/iidr/report.html`.

[55] M.M. Fleck, D. A. Forsyth, and C. Bregler. Finding naked people. In *Proceedings of the ECCV*, volume 2, pages 593–602, 1996.

[56] R.M. Ford, C. Robson, D. Temple, and M. Gerlach. Metrics for scene change detection in digital video sequences. In *Proceedings of International Conference on Multimedia Systems*, pages 610–611, 1997.

[57] D.A. Forsyth and M.M. Fleck. Body plans. In *Proceedings of the IEEE Conference on Computer Vision and Pattern Recognition*, pages 678–683, 1997.

[58] E. Fredkin. Trie memory. *Communications of the ACM*, 3:490–499, 1960.

[59] B. Funt and G. Fianlayson. Color constant color indexing. *IEEE Transactions on Pattern Analysis and Machine Intelligence*, 17(5):522–529, 1995.

[60] T. Gevers and A. W. M. Smeulders. The PicToSeek WWW image search system. In *Proceedings of the International Conference on Multimedia Computing and Systems*, Florence, Italy, 1999.

[61] T. Gevers and A.W.M. Smeulders. PicToSeek: combining color and shape invariant features for image retrieval. *IEEE Transactions on Image Processing*, 9(1):102–119, January 2000.

[62] E.B. Goldstein. *Sensation & Perception*. Brooks/Cole, Pacific Grove, CA, 1999.

[63] Y. Gong. Automatic parsing of TV soccer programs. In *Proceedings of 2nd International Conference on Multimedia Computing and Systems*, pages 167–174, May 1995.

[64] Y. Gong. *Intelligent Image Databases: towards advanced image retrieval.* Kluwer Academic Publishers, Boston, 1998.

[65] Y. Gong, G. Proietti, and C. Faloutsos. Image indexing and retrieval based on human perceptual color clustering. In *Proceedings in IEEE Computer Society Conference on Computer Vision and Pattern Recognition*, pages 578–583, 1998.

[66] R. C. Gonzalez and R. E Woods. *Digital Image Processing.* Prentice-Hall, Upper Saddle River, NJ, 2nd edition, 2002.

[67] P.O. Gresle and T.S. Huang. Gisting of video documents: a key frames selection algorithm using relative activity measure. In *Proceedings of 2nd International Conference on Visual Information Systems*, pages 279–286, 1997.

[68] L. Grewe and A. C. Kak. Interactive learning of a multi-attribute hash table classifier for fast object recognition. *Computer Vision and Image Understanding*, 61(3):387–416, 1995.

[69] W. I. Grosky. Multimedia information systems. *IEEE Multimedia*, 1(1):12–24, 1994.

[70] W. I. Grosky, R. Jain, and R. Mehrotra, editors. *The Handbook of Multimedia Information Management*. Prentice Hall, 1997.

[71] M. H. Gross, R. Koch, L. Lippert, and A. Dreger. Multiscale image texture analysis in wavelet spaces. In *Proc. IEEE International Conference on Image Processing*, volume 3, pages 412–416, Austin, TX, USA, November 1994.

[72] V. N. Gudivada and V. V. Raghavan. Content-based image retrieval systems. *IEEE Computer*, 28(9):18–31, September 1995.

[73] A. Gupta and R. Jain. Visual information retrieval. *Communications of the ACM*, 40(5):71–79, May 1997.

[74] A. Gupta, S. Santini, and R. Jain. In search of information in visual media. *Communications of the ACM*, 40(12):35–42, December 1997.

[75] A. Guttmann. R-trees: A dynamic index structure for spatial searching. In *Proceedings of ACM-SIGMOD*, pages 47–57, 1984.

[76] A. Hampapur, R. Jain, and T. E Weymouth. Digital video segmentation. In *Proceedings of the second ACM international conference on Multimedia '94*, pages 357–364, San Francisco, CA, 1994.

[77] A. Hampapur, R. Jain, and T. E. Weymouth. Production model based digital video segmentation. In B. Furht, editor, *Multimedia Tools and Applications*, chapter 4. Kluwer Academic Publishers, Boston, 1996.

[78] J. Han and M. Kamber. *Data mining: concepts and techniques*. Morgan Kaufmann, San Francisco, 2001.

[79] A. Hanjalic and R.L. Lagendijk. A new key-frame allocation method for representing sotred video streams. In *Proceedings of the 1st International Workshop on Image Databases and Multimedia Search*, Amsterdam, 1996.

[80] R. Haralick, K. Shanmugam, and I. Dinstein. Texture features for image classification. *IEEE Transactions on Systems, Man, and Cybernetics*, 3(6), 1973.

[81] K. Hirata, Y. Hara, N. Shibata, and F. Hirabayashi. Media-based navigation for hypermedia systems. In *Proceedings of the fifth ACM conference on Hypertext, November 14-18, '93, Seattle, WA, USA*, pages 159–173, 1993.

[82] K. Hirata, S. Mukherjea, W.-S. Li, and Y. Hara. Integrating image matching and classification for multimedia retrieval on the web. In *Proceedings of the*

International Conference on Multimedia Computing and Systems, volume 1, pages 257–263, Florence, Italy, 1999.

[83] K. Hirata, S. Mukherjea, Y. Okamura, W.-S. Li, and Y. Hara. Object-based navigation: An intuitive navigation style for content-oriented integration environment. In *Proceedings of the eighth ACM conference on Hypertext, '97, Southampton, UK*, pages 75–86, 1997. `http://journals.ecs.soton.ac.uk/~lac/ht97/`.

[84] M. Hu. Visual pattern recognition by moment invariants. *IRE Transactions on Information Theory*, IT-8:179–182, 1962.

[85] J. Huang. *Color-spatial Image Indexing and Applications*. PhD thesis, Cornell University, 1998.

[86] J. Huang, S. Kumar, M. Mitra, W.-J. Zhu, and R. Zabih. Image indexing using color correlograms. In *Proc. IEEE International Conference on Computer Vision and Pattern Recognition*, pages 762–768, San Juan, Puerto Rico, 1997.

[87] D. P. Huijsmans and A. W. M. Smeulders, editors. *Visual Information and Information Systems, Proceedings of the Third International Conference VISUAL '99, Amsterdam, The Netherlands, June 1999*, Lecture Notes in Computer Science 1614. Springer, 1999.

[88] D. W. Jacobs, D. Weinshall, and Y. Gdalyahu. Condensing image databases when retrieval is based on non-metric distances. In *Proc. 6th International Conference on Computer Vision*, pages 596–601, 1998.

[89] R. Jain. Infoscopes: Multimedia information system. In B. Furht, editor, *Multimedia Systems and Techniques*, pages 217–253. Kluwer, 1996.

[90] R. Kasturi and R. Jain. Dynamic visions. In *Proceedings of Computer Vision:Principles*, Washington, 1991. IEEE Computers Society Prees.

[91] L. Kaufman and P.J. Rousseeuw. *Finding Groups in Data: an introduction to cluster analysis*. Wiley, 1990.

[92] P. M. Kelly, T. M. Cannon, and D. R. Hush. Query by image example: the CANDID approach. In *SPIE Vol. 2420, Storage and Retrieval for Image and Video Databases III*, pages 238–248, 1995.

[93] I. Konigsberg. *The Complete Film Dictionary - 2nd ed.* Penguin, New York, 1997.

[94] H. F. Korth and A. Silberschatz. *Database System Concepts*. McGraw-Hill, 1991.

[95] S. Krishnamachari and M. Abdel-Mottaleb. Image browsing using hierarchical clustering. In *Proceedings of the IEEE International Symposium on Computers and Communications*, pages 301–307, 1999.

[96] A. Kuchinsky et al. Fotofile: a consumer multimedia organization and retrieval system. In *Proceeding of the CHI 99 conference on Human factors in computing systems: the CHI is the limit*, Pittsburgh, PA, USA, 1999.

[97] M. La Cascia and E. Ardizzone. JACOB: Just a content-based query system for video databases. In *Proceedings IEEE International Conference on Acoustics, Speech, and Signal Processing*, volume 2, pages 1216–1219, Atlanta, Georgia, May 1996.

[98] J. Laaksonen, M. Koskela, S. Laakso, and E. Oja. PicSOM - content-based image retrieval with self-organizing maps. *Pattern Recognition Letters*, 21:1199–1207, 2000.

[99] T.-S. Lai. *CHROMA: a Photographic Image Retrieval System*. PhD thesis, School of Computing, Engineering and Technology, University of Sunderland, UK, January 2000. http://osiris.sund.ac.uk/~cs0sla/thesis/.

[100] A. Laine and J. Fan. Texture classification by wavelet packet signatures. *IEEE Transactions on Pattern Analysis and Machine Intelligence*, 15(11), 1993.

[101] C.H.C. Leung and H.H.S. Ip. Benchmarking for content-based visual information search. http://www.cs.addressu.edu.hk/~leung/TC-12/Benchmark8.doc.

[102] M. Lew, K. Lempinen, and N. Huijmans. Webcrawling using sketches. In *Proceedings of the 2nd International Conference on Visual Information Systems, San Diego, December '97*, pages 77–84, 1997.

[103] M. S. Lew, D. P. Huijsmans, and D. Denteneer. Content based image retrieval: KLT, projections, or templates. In Smeulders and Jain [151], pages 27–34.

[104] Z. N. Li, O. R. Zaïane, and B. Yan. C-bird: Content-based image retrieval from image repositories using chromatiaddress and recognition kernel. Technical Report CMPT98-03, School of Computing Science, Simon Fraser University, Canada, February 1998. ftp://ftp.fas.sfu.ca/pub/cs/TR/1998/CMPT1998-03.ps.gz.

[105] Z.N. Li, O. R. Zaïane, and Z. Tauber. Illumination invariance and object model in content-based image and video retrieval. *Journal of Visual Communication and Image Representation*, 10(3):219–244, September 1999. http://www.cs.sfu.ca/cs/undergrad/CM/CMPT365/CBS/CBIRD.pdf.

[106] LTU technologies. http://www.ltutech.com.

[107] W. Y. Ma. *NETRA: A Toolbox for Navigating Large Image Databases*. PhD thesis, Dept. of Electrical and Computer Engineering, University of California at Santa Barbara, June 1997.

[108] W.-Y. Ma and B. S. Manjunath. Netra: A toolbox for navigating large image databases. *Multimedia Systems*, 7(3):184–198, 1999.

[109] W. Y. Ma and B.S. Manjunath. Netra: a toolbox for navigating large image databases. In *Proceedings of the IEEE International Conference on Image Processing*, volume 1, pages 568–571, October 1997.

[110] B. S. Manjunath. Image browsing in the alexandria digital library project. *D-Lib Magazine*, page http://www.dlib.org/dlib/august95/alexandria/08manjunath.html, August 1995.

[111] R. Manmatha and S. Ravela. A syntactic characterization of appearance and its application to image retrieval. In *Proceedings of the SPIE conference on Human Vision and Electronic Imaging II, Vol. 3016, San Jose, CA, Feb. '97*, 1997.

[112] C. Meilhac and C. Nastar. Relevance feedback and category search in image databases. In *Proceedings of the International Conference on Multimedia Computing and Systems*, volume 1, pages 512–517, Florence, Italy, 1999.

[113] J. Meng, F. Juan, and S.-F. Chang. Scene change detection in a mpeg compressed video sequence. In *Symposium on Electronic Imaging: Science & Technology*, volume 2417, pages 1–12, San Jose, February 1995.

[114] S. Michel, B. Karoubi, J. Bigun, and S. Corsini. Orientation radiograms for indexing and identification in image databases. In *Proceedings Eusipco-96, European conference on signal processing*, pages 1693–1696, 1996.

[115] T. J. Mills, D. Pye, D. Sinclair, and K. R. Wood. Shoebox: A digital photo management system. Technical Report Technical Report 2000.10, AT&T Research, `http://ftp.uk.research.att.com:/pub/docs/att/tr.2000.10.pdf/`, 2000.

[116] T. Minka. An image database browser that learns from user interaction. MEng thesis, MIT, 1996.

[117] T. P. Minka and R. Picard. Interactive learning using a "society of models". Technical Report 349, MIT Media Laboratory Perceptual Computing Section, 1995.

[118] B. Moghaddam and A. Pentland. Bayesian image retrieval in biometric databases. In *Proceedings of the International Conference on Multimedia Computing and Systems*, volume 2, pages 610–615, Florence, Italy, 1999.

[119] F. Mokhtarian, S. Abbasi, and J. Kittler. Efficient and robust retrieval by shape content through curvature scale space. In Smeulders and Jain [151], pages 35–42.

[120] S. Mukherjea, K. Hirata, and Y. Hara. Towards a multimedia world wide web information retrieval engine. In *Sixth International WWW Conference, 7-11 April '97, Santa Clara, CA, USA*, 1997. `http://decweb.ethz.ch/WWW6/Technical/Paper003/Paper3.html`.

[121] S. Mukherjea, K. Hirata, and Y. Hara. AMORE: A world wide web image retrieval engine. *The WWW Journal*, 2(3):115–132, 1999. `http://www.baltzer.nl/www/contents/1999/2-3.html`.

[122] A. Nagasaka and Y. Tanaka. Automatic video indexing and full-search for video appearances. In E. Knuth and I.M. Wegener, editors, *Visual Database Systems 2*, pages 113–127. Elsevier Science Publishers, Amstredam, 1992.

[123] M.R. Naphade, R. Mehrotra, A.M. Fermant, J. Warnick, T.S. Huang, and A.M. Tekalp. A high-performance shot boundary detection algorithm using multiple cues. In *Proceedings of International Conference on Image Processing*, volume 1, pages 884–887, 1998.

[124] C. Nastar, M. Mitschke, C. Meilhac, and N. Boujemaa. Surfimage: A flexible content-based image retrieval system. In *Proceedings of the ACM International Multimedia Conference, 12-16 September '98, Bristol, England*, pages 339–344, 1998. `http://www-rocq.inria.fr/_nastar/MM98/`.

[125] W. Niblack, R. Barber, W. Equitz, M. Flickner, E. Glasman, D. Petkovic, P. Yanker, C. Faloutsos, and G. Taubin. The QBIC project: Querying images by content using color, texture and shape. In *Proc. SPIE Storage and Retrieval for Image and Video Databases*, pages 173–187, San Jose, February 1993.

[126] V.E. Ogle and M. Stonebraker. Chabot: retrieval from a relational database of images. *IEEE Computer*, 28(9):40–48, September 1995.

[127] J. Oh, K. Hua, and N. Liang. A content-based scene change detection and classification technique using background tracking. In *Proceedings of the SPIE Conf. on Multimedia Computing and Networking 2000*, San Jose, CA, January 2000.

[128] N. Oliver. *Towards Perceptual Intelligence: Statistical Modeling of Human Individual and Interactive Behaviors.* PhD thesis, MIT, 2000.

[129] M. Ortega, Y. Rui, K. Chakrabarti, S. Mehrotra, and T. S. Huang. Supporting similarity queries in MARS. In *Proceedings of the 5th ACM International Multimedia Conference, Seattle, Washington, 8-14 Nov. '97*, pages 403–413, 1997.

[130] P. Pala and S. Santini. Image retrieval by shape and texture. *Pattern Recognition*, 32(3):517–527, 1999.

[131] G. Pass, R. Zabih, and J. Miller. Comparing images using color coherence vectors. In *Proc. ACM Conference on Multimedia*, pages 65–73, Boston, MA, 1996.

[132] A. Pentland, R. W. Picard, and S. Sclaroff. Photobook: Content-based manipulation of image databases. In B. Furht, editor, *Multimedia Tools and Applications*, chapter 2. Kluwer Academic Publishers, Boston, MA, 1996.

[133] J.C. Platt. AutoAlbum: Clustering digital photographs using probabistic model merging. In *Proc. IEEE Workshop on Content-Based Access of Image and Video Libraries*, pages 96–100, Hilton Head Island, SC, USA, 2000.

[134] A. Rosenfeld and E.B. Troy. Visual texture analysis. In *Conf. Record for Symposium on Feature Extraction and Selection in Pattern Recognition*, pages 115–124, 1970.

[135] Y. Rui, T. S. Huang, and S.-F. Chang. Image retrieval: Current techniques, promising directions and open issues. *Journal of Visual Communication and Image Representation*, 10(1):1–23, March 1999.

[136] Y. Rui, T. S. Huang, and S. Mehrotra. Content-based image retrieval with relevance feedback in MARS. In *Proceedings of IEEE Int. Conf. Image Processing*, pages 815–818, 1997.

[137] Y. Rui, T. S. Huang, S. Mehrotra, and M. Ortega. Automatic matching tool selection using relevance feedback in MARS. In *Proc. 2nd Int. Conf. Visual Information Systems*, pages 109–116, 1997.

[138] Y. Rui, T. S. Huang, S. Mehrotra, and M. Ortega. A relevance feedback architecture for content-based multimedia information retrieval systems. In *Proceedings of IEEE Workshop on Content-based Access of Image and Video Libraries*, pages 82–89, 1997.

[139] Y. Rui, T. S. Huang, M. Ortega, and S. Mehrotra. Relevance feedback: A power tool for interactive content-based image retrieval. *IEEE Transactions on Circuits and Systems for Video Technology*, 8(5):644–655, 1998.

[140] Y. Rui and T.S. Huang. Unified framework for video browsing and retrieval. In A. Bovik, editor, *Handbook of Image and Video Processing*, chapter 9.2. Academic Press, San Diego, 2000.

[141] Y. Rui, T.S. Huang, and S Mehrotra. Relevance feedback techniques in interactive content-based image retrieval. In *Proc. S&T SPIE Storage and Retrieval of Images/ Video Databases VI, EI'98*, 1998.

[142] S. Sclaroff, L. Taycher, and M. La Cascia. ImageRover: A content-based image browser for the world wide web. In *Proceedings IEEE Workshop on Content-based Access of Image and Video Libraries, June '97*, pages 2–9, San Juan, Puerto Rico, 1997.

[143] T. Sellis, N. Roussopoulos, and C. Faloutsos. The r+-tree: A dynamic index for multi-dimensional objects. In *Proceeding of the* 13th *International Conference on Very Large Data Bases*, pages 507–518, Brighton, 1987.

[144] I. K. Sethi and N. V Patel. A statistical approach to scene change detection. In *Proc. of the IS&T/SPIE Symposium on Electronic Imaging Science and Technology, Conference on Storage and Retrieval for Image and Video Databases III*, San Jose, 1995.

[145] B. Shahraray. Scene change detection and content-based sampling of video sequences. In *Proceedings of SPIE Conference on Digital Video Compression: Algorithm and Technologies*, volume 2419, pages 2–13, San Jose, February 1995.

[146] L.G. Shapiro and G.C. Stockman. *Computer Vision*. Prentice-Hall, Upper Saddle River, NJ, 2001.

[147] G. Sheikholeslami, W. Chang, and A. Zhang. Semantic clustering and querying on heterogeneous features for visual data. In *Proceedings of the* 6th *ACM International Multimedia Conference*, pages 3–12, Bristol, England, 1998.

[148] J.-C. Shim, C. Dorai, and R. Bolle. Automatic text extraction from video for content-based annotation and retrieval. Technical Report RC 21087 94340, IBM T.J. Watson Research Center, 1998.

[149] C.-R. Shyu, C. E. Brodley, A. C. Kak, A. Kosaka, A. Aisen, and L. Broderick. Assert: A physician-in-the-loop content-based retrieval system for HRCT image databases. *Computer Vision and Image Understanding*, 75(1/2):111–132, July/August 1999.

[150] S. Siggelkow and H. Burkhardt. Fast invariant feature extraction for image retrieval. In R. C. Veltkamp, H. Burkhardt, and H.-P. Kriegel, editors, *State-of-the-Art in Content-Based Image and Video Retrieval.* Kluwer, 2001.

[151] A. W. M. Smeulders and R. Jain, editors. *Image Databases and Multi-Media Search, proceedings of the First International Workshop IDB-MMS'96, Amsterdam, The Netherlands.* Amsterdam University Press, August 1996.

[152] J. R. Smith. *Integrated Spatial and Feature Image Systems: Retrieval, Compression and Analysis.* PhD thesis, Graduate School of Arts and Sciences, Columbia University, February 1997.

[153] J. R. Smith. Videozoom spatio-temporal video browser. *IEEE Transactions on Multimedia*, 1(2), 1999.

[154] J. R. Smith and S.-F. Chang. Automated image retrieval using color and texture. Technical Report CU/CTR 408-95-14, CTR, Columbia University, July 1995.

[155] J. R. Smith and S.-F. Chang. Single color extraction and image query. In *Proc. IEEE International Conference on Image Processing*, volume 3, pages 528–531, Washington, DC, 1995.

[156] J. R. Smith and S.-F. Chang. VisualSEEk: a fully automated content-based image query system. In *Proc. ACM Multimedia*, Boston, MA, November 1996.

[157] J.R. Smith and S.-F Chang. Tools and techniques for color image retrieval. In *Proc. SPIE Conference on Storage and Retrieval for Image and Video Database IV, 2670*, San Jose, CA, february 1996.

[158] J.R. Smith and S-F. Chang. Querying by color regions using the visualSEEk content-based visual query system. In M. T. Maybury, editor, *Intelligent Multimedia Information Retrieval*, chapter 2, pages 23–41. American Association for Artificial Intelligence AAAI, Menlo Park, CA, 1997.

[159] M. A. Smith and T. Kanade. Video skinmming and characterization through the combination of image and language understanding techniques. Technical Report CMU-CS-97-11, Carnegie Mellon University, February 1997.

[160] S. W. Smoliar and H.-J. Zhang. Content-based video indexing and retrieval. *IEEE Multimedia*, 1(2), 1994.

[161] R. Srihari. Automatic indexing and content-based retrieval of captioned images. *IEEE Computer*, 28(9):49–56, September 1995.

[162] R. Srihari, Z. Zhang, and A. Rao. Intelligent indexing and semantic retrieval of multimodal documents. *Information Retrieval*, 2(2):245–275, 2000. `http://www.cse.buffalo.edu/~arao/Papers/ir.ps.gz`.

[163] M. Stricker and M. Orengo. Similarity of color images. In *Proc. SPIE Storage and Retrieval for Image and Video Databases*, 1995.

[164] M. J. Swain, C. Frankel, and V. Athitsos. WebSeer: An image search engine for the world wide web. Technical Report TR-96-14, Deptartment of Computer Science, University of Chicago, July 1996.

[165] M.J. Swain and D.H. Ballard. Indexing via color histograms. In *Proc. Third International Conference on Computer Vision*, pages 390–393, 1990.

[166] M.J. Swain and D.H. Ballard. Color indexing. *International Journal of Computer Vision*, 7:11–32, 1991.

[167] D. Swanberg, C.F. Shu, and R Jain. Knowledge guided parsing in video databases. In *Storage and Retrieval for Image and Video Databases, SPIE*, volume 1908, pages 13–25, Feb 1993.

[168] M. Szummer and R.W. Picard. Indoor-outdoor image classification. In *Workshop in Content-based Access to Image and Video Databases*, pages 42–51, 1998.

[169] H. Tamura, S. Mori, and T. Yamawaki. Texture features corresponding to visual perception. *IEEE Transactions on Systems, Man and Cybernetics*, 8(6):460–473, 1978.

[170] H. Tamura and N. Yokoya. Image database systems: A survey. *Pattern Recognition*, 17(1):29–43, 1984.

[171] Y. Taniguchi, A. Akutsu, and Y. Tonomura. Panorama excerpts: Extracting and packing panoramas for videeo browsing. In *Proceedings of the 5th ACM International Multimedia Conference*, pages 427–436, Seattle, December 1997.

[172] L. Taycher, M. La Cascia, and S. Sclaroff. Image digestion and relevance feedback in the ImageRover WWW search engine. In *Proceedings of the 2nd International Conference on Visual Information Systems, San Diego, December '97*, pages 85–94, 1997.

[173] L. Teodosio and W. Bender. Salient video stills: Content and context preserved. In *Proc. ACM Multimedia*, pages 39–46, Anaheim, California, 1993.

[174] Y. Tonomura, A. Akutsu, Y. Taniguchi, and G. Suzuki. Structured video computing. *IEEE Multimedia*, 1(3):34–43, 1994.

[175] N. Vasconcelos and A Lippman. Bayesian relevance feedback for content-based image retrieval. In *Proc. IEEE Workshop on Content-Based Access of Image and Video Libraries*, pages 63–67, 2000.

[176] N. Vasconcelos and A. Lippman. Statistical models of video structure for content analysis and characterization. *IEEE Transactions on Image Processing*, 9(1):3–19, January 2000.

[177] R. C. Veltkamp and M. Hagedoorn. State-of-the-art in shape matching. In Michael Lew, editor, *Principles of Visual Information Retrieval*, pages 87–119. Springer, 2001.

[178] J. Vendrig. Filter image browsing: a study to image retrieval in large pictorial databases. Master's thesis, Dept. Computer Science, University of Amsterdam, The Netherlands, `http://carol.wins.uva.nl/~vendrig/thesis/`, February 1997.

[179] J. Vendrig, M. Worring, and A. W. M. Smeulders. Filter image browsing: Exploiting interaction in image retrieval. In Huijsmans and Smeulders [87], pages 147–154.

[180] J. Vleugels and R. C. Veltkamp. Efficient image retrieval through vantage objects. *Pattern Recognition*, 35(1):69–80, 2002.

[181] S. Volmer. Tracing images in large databases by comparison of wavelet fingerprints. In *Proceedings of the 2nd International Conference on Visual Information Systems, San Diego, December '97*, pages 163–172, 1997.

[182] J. Wang, T.-S. Chua, and L. Chen. Cinematic-based model for scene boundary detection. In *Proceedings of MMM2001 (Multimedia Modeling Conference)*, Amsterdam, November 2001.

[183] J. Z. Wang, G. Wiederhold, O. Firschein, and S. X. Wei. Wavelet-based image indexing techniques with partial sketch retrieval capability. In *Proceedings of the Fourth Forum on Research and Technology Advances in Digital Libraries, Washington D.C., May '97*, pages 13–24, 1997. `http://www-db.stanford.edu/~wangz/project/imsearch/ADL97/`.

[184] Z. Wang, L. Hill, and T. Smith. Alexandria digital library metadata creator with extensible markup language. In *Proceedings of the Third International Conference on Conceptions of Library and Information Science (CoLIS 3). Digital Libraries: Interdisciplinary Concepts, Challenges and Opportunities. Dubrovnik, Croatia*, 1999.

[185] D.A. White and R. Jain. Similarity indexing: Algorithms and performance. In *Proceedings of SPIE Storage and Retrieval for Image and Video Databases IV*, volume 70, pages 62–75, San Jose, CA, 1996.

[186] D.A. White and R. Jain. Similarity indexing with the SS-tree. In *Proceedings of the 12th IEEE International Conference on Data Engineering*, pages 516–523, New Orleans, 1996.

[187] I.H. Witten and E. Frank. *Data mining: practical machine learning tools and techniques with Java implementations.* Morgan Kaufmann, San Francisco, 2000.

[188] W. Wolf. Key frame selection by motion analysis. In *Proceedings of the IEEE International Conference on Visual Information Systems*, pages 1228–1231, Atlanta, May 1996.

[189] B.-L. Yeo. *Efficient Processing of Compressed Images and Video.* PhD thesis, Princeton University, 1996.

[190] B. L. Yeo and B. Liu. Rapid scene analysis on compressed videos. *IEEE Trans. Circuits Syst. Video Technology*, 5(6):533–544, 1995.

[191] M. Yeung, B.-L. Yeo, and B. Liu. Extracting story units from long programs for video browsing and navigation. In *Proceedings of the International Conference on Multimedia Computing and Systems*, pages 296–305, 1996.

[192] M. M. Yeung and B. L. Yeo. Video visualization for compact representation and fast browsing of pictorial content. *IEEE Trans. Circuits Syst. Video Technology*, 7(5):771–785, 1997.

[193] Z. Yongwei. Development of a video database system with content-based indexing and retrieval capabilities. Master's thesis, Nanyang Technological University, 1998.

[194] R. Zabih, K. Mai, and J. Miller. A robust method for detecting cuts and dissolves in video sequences. In *Proceedings of the ACM 3rd Internationl Multimedia Conference*, pages 189–200, November 1995.

[195] H.-J Zhang. Content-based video browsing and retrieval. In B. Furht, editor, *Handbook of Internet and Multimedia Systems and Applications*, chapter 712. CRC Press, Boca Raton, 1999.

[196] H.-J. Zhang. Content-based video browsing and retrieval. In K. Jeffay and H.-J. Zhang, editors, *Readings in Multimedia Computing and Networking*, chapter 5. Morgan Kaufmann, San Francisco, 2002.

[197] H.-J. Zhang et al. Video parsing using compressed data. In *Proceedings of SPIE conference on Image and Video Processing 2*, pages 142–149, February 1994.

[198] H.-J. Zhang, A. Kankanhalli, and S.W Smoliar. Automatic partitioning of full-motion video. *ACM Multimedia Systems*, 1(1):10–28, 1993.

[199] H.-J. Zhang, C.Y Low, S.W. Smoliar, and D. Zhong. Video parsing, retrieval and browsing: An integrated and content-based solution. In *Proceedings of ACM conference on Multimedia*, pages 15–24, San Fransisco, November 1995.

[200] H.-J. Zhang, S. Tan, S. Smoliar, and G. Yihong. Automatic parsing and indexing of news video. *Multimedia Systems*, 2:256–266, 1995.

[201] D. Zhong, H.-J. Zhang, and S.-F. Chang. Clustering methods for video browsing and annotation. In *Proceedings of the SPIE Conference on Storage and Retrieval for Image and Video Databases 4*, volume 2670, pages 239–246, San Jose, February 1996.

[202] Y. Zhuang, Y. Rui, T.S. Huang, and S. Mehrotra. Adaptive key frame extraction using unsupervised clustering. In *Proceedings of the IEEE International Conference on Image Processing*, volume 1, pages 866–870, Chicago, October 1998.

About the Authors

Oge Marques is an Assistant Professor in the Department of Computer Science and Engineering at Florida Atlantic University in Boca Raton, Florida. He received his B.S. degree in Electrical Engineering from *Centro Federal de Educação Tecnológica do Paraná* (CEFET-PR) in Curitiba, Brazil, a Master's degree in Electronic Engineering from Philips International Institute of Technological Studies in Eindhoven, The Netherlands, and a Ph.D. degree in Computer Engineering from Florida Atlantic University. Dr. Marques has several recent publications, including the coauthorship of a textbook in Digital Image Processing (in Portuguese), book chapters, journal and conference papers, and technical reports on topics ranging from video databases to Web-based learning. His current fields of interest include visual information retrieval, digital image processing, video databases, and computer networks.

Borko Furht is a professor of computer science and engineering at Florida Atlantic University (FAU) in Boca Raton, Florida. He is the founder and director of the Multimedia Laboratory at FAU, funded by National Science Foundation. Before joining FAU, he was a vice president of research and a senior director of development at Modcomp, a computer company of Daimler Benz, Germany, a professor at University of Miami in Coral Gables, Florida, and senior scientist at Institute "Boris Kidric"-Vinca, Belgrade, Yugoslavia. He received Ph.D., MSEE, and B.Sc. (Dipl. Eng.) degrees from the University of Belgrade, Yugoslavia. He has published numerous scientific and technical papers, books, and holds several patents. He received research grants from NSF, NASA, IBM, Xerox, and Racal Datacom. His research interests include multimedia systems and applications, video coding and retrieval, and Internet engineering.

Index

GPSR Compliance

The European Union's (EU) General Product Safety Regulation (GPSR) is a set of rules that requires consumer products to be safe and our obligations to ensure this.

If you have any concerns about our products, you can contact us on ProductSafety@springernature.com

In case Publisher is established outside the EU, the EU authorized representative is:

Springer Nature Customer Service Center GmbH
Europaplatz 3
69115 Heidelberg, Germany

Batch number: 10755292

Printed by Printforce, the Netherlands